T0038427

PRAISE FOR

This Hallelujah Banquet

"If you've ever wondered what the book of Revelation could possibly have to do with your life now, you're not alone. Eugene Peterson asked the same question, and then he brought us the message of *This Hallelujah Banquet.* This is a wonderfully practical guide for finding joy and peace in a world that is sometimes anything but. Read it and be blessed."

—MARK BATTERSON, *New York Times*
bestselling author of *The Circle Maker* and
lead pastor of National Community Church

"In *This Hallelujah Banquet,* with Eugene Peterson as an expert tour guide, we step into the book of Revelation. He wisely urges readers to resist the temptation to turn Revelation into a road map toward future chaos. Instead, he shows us how to navigate the world of seven first-century churches to notice the parallels between their struggles and our own. I highly recommend this book to anyone who desires to live as though the banquet with Jesus has already begun. Transformative, prophetic in the best way, and timely!"

—KURT WILLEMS, pastor, podcast host,
and author of *Echoing Hope*

"The last book of the Bible is a revelation of Jesus Christ, but it is also a revelation from Jesus about the state of the world and the condition of the church. Peterson's sermons on the seven letters to the seven churches speak to us about how we love, suffer, tell the truth, cultivate holiness, perceive reality, bear witness, and persist in commitment. Insightful and inviting, each chapter calls us to examine our lives so that we might endure till the end. This is Eugene at his pastoral best."

—REV. DR. GLENN PACKIAM, associate senior pastor at New Life Church and author of *Blessed Broken Given*

"They say the power of a sermon is not only in what it tells but in how it transports. The sermons carefully captured in this book still retain that kind of transformative power, even in written form and years after they were first preached. *This Hallelujah Banquet* invites us to a place where Eugene Peterson's warm and challenging words are still alive and proclaiming good news."

—MANDY SMITH, pastor and author of *Unfettered* and *The Vulnerable Pastor*

"Anyone who has read Eugene Peterson's work knows that his pen pulses with the energy of the Spirit. And he brings some of his best work to bear on the last book in the Bible—Saint John's Revelation. For far too long, this book has been preached as if it's bad news. But Eugene reclaims it by helping us rediscover the good news that's crackling on every page. So take this book and read it!"

—DANIEL GROTHE, associate senior pastor at New Life Church

THIS
HALLELUJAH
BANQUET

THIS

HALLELUJAH
BANQUET

How the End of What We Were
Reveals Who We Can Be

EUGENE H. PETERSON

WATERBROOK

THIS HALLELUJAH BANQUET

Published in the United States by WaterBrook, an imprint of Random House, a division of Penguin Random House LLC.

WATERBROOK® and its deer colophon are registered trademarks of Penguin Random House LLC.

Published in association with the literary agency of Alive Literary Agency, Colorado Springs, Colorado, www.aliveliterary.com.

Library of Congress Cataloging-in-Publication Data
Names: Peterson, Eugene H., 1932–2018, author.
Title: This hallelujah banquet : how the end of what we were reveals who we can be / Eugene H. Peterson.
Description: First edition. | Colorado Springs : WaterBrook, 2021.
Identifiers: LCCN 2020020781 | ISBN 9781601429858 (hardcover : acid-free paper) | ISBN 9781601429865 (ebook)
Subjects: LCSH: Bible. Revelation—Criticism, interpretation, etc.
Classification: LCC BS2825.52 .P485 2021 | DDC 228/.06—dc23
LC record available at https://lccn.loc.gov/2020020781

Printed in the United States of America on acid-free paper

waterbrookmultnomah.com

2 4 6 8 9 7 5 3

Images on title page, part pages, and Final Exams: copyright © iStock.com/Jobalou

Book design by Victoria Wong

SPECIAL SALES
Most WaterBrook books are available at special quantity discounts when purchased in bulk by corporations, organizations, and special-interest groups. Custom imprinting or excerpting can also be done to fit special needs. For information, please email specialmarketscms@penguinrandomhouse.com.

Contents

✳

Contents

Editor's Note

This Hallelujah Banquet was created primarily from a sermon series that Eugene H. Peterson preached at Christ Our King Presbyterian Church in Bel Air, Maryland, during Lent in 1984, along with wider commentary and materials from his personal archives.

We at WaterBrook have selected and edited this material to read smoothly while remaining faithful to Eugene's unique voice and pastoral intention. Our edits and additions have been limited. Besides correction of minor errors and some reordering for flow and clarity, the only changes have been to remove dated references (to technology, politics, pop culture, and so forth), replacing those with the principles Eugene was making, and to add related material from other work on Revelation in places where additional context is helpful in a printed setting. (For example, much of the opening chapter of the book—which gives valuable insight into Eugene's thoughts on John's ministry to the churches of Revelation and our need to return to these words of Christ through John—came from a much earlier 1967 sermon.) As well, we occasionally have inserted a few especially profound insights from his later writings on Revelation in places where they fit naturally with his earlier preaching.

We have strived to take no unnecessary liberties with Eugene's words or thoughts and to present them to you with the craft and care that Eugene exercised in writing and preaching them. Speaking personally, as I have worked, I have noted with pleasure the special intimacy that comes from words meant to be spoken. I think Eugene would have smiled to see his sermons still "preaching" after so many years of Sundays.

A final structural note: each of the letters follows a similar outline. First, Christ presents a particular part of his character. Next, Christ examines the Christians. The examination reveals both strengths and weaknesses, and so corrective action is commanded. An urgent promise concludes each message. Far from a wooden devotion to this approach, Eugene honors its rhythm in each of the chapters. In these messages, we are confronted with how the end of one way of life—or even one version of our faith—can usher in a new and more vibrant connection with Christ. Every ending can become a beginning. It is this theme of examination and invitation that forms the core of Eugene's teaching in this book.

When this book was first pulled together in the fall of 2019, we had no idea of the global changes that would come with the widespread pandemic of 2020. Now, as it releases at the beginning of a misty 2021, a sober attentiveness has come. More than anytime in living memory, it has felt for many like the end of the world. With that have come grief, reflection, and hope—all of which are present in these pages.

It's with quiet joy and expectation that we at Water-Brook, with the blessing of Eugene's family, present this special book to you. May it lead you to a deeper knowledge of the Lamb, who invites us all to his eternal feast, to this rich and timely hallelujah banquet.

—PAUL J. PASTOR, editor

BEGINNING
AT THE END

He who sat upon the throne said,
"Behold, I make all things new." Also
he said, "Write this, for these words
are trustworthy and true." And he
said to me, "It is done! I am the
Alpha and the Omega, the beginning
and the end. To the thirsty I will give
from the fountain of the water of life
without payment. He who conquers
shall have this heritage, and I will be
his God and he shall be my son."

—Revelation 21:5–7

The End Is Where We Start

The last book of the Bible, Revelation, has some of the best words to start the year, words that launch us into the pages of our calendars.[*] T. S. Eliot wrote in "Little Gidding,"

> What we call the beginning is often the end
> And to make an end is to make a beginning.
> The end is where we start from.[†]

"The end is where we start from." The end of the Bible is the beginning of our new year's existence. It

---

[*] Editor's note: This chapter was originally preached as a New Year's sermon. Though I've retained Eugene's language about the beginning of the calendar year, this teaching gives fitting context for the wisdom Revelation carries for any new beginning.

[†] T. S. Eliot, "Little Gidding," *Four Quartets* (New York: Harcourt, 1943), 42.

functions for us in this way as it speaks to our mood and condition.

The characteristic mood, the typical mental stance, on New Year's Day is a look to the future. We have a calendar of unused days stretching out before us. There is curiosity about them and fear of them. Amateur prophets make predictions. Astrological magazines and horoscope plotters are in their peak season. Articles proliferate in magazines and newspapers: the business outlook, the literary prospects, the political probabilities, the social changes expected. And with all this, no one can avoid these personal questions: What will it bring for me? What waits to be recorded in the diary pages of the new year?

The book of Revelation is the word of God that speaks to this combination of anxiety and hope about the future. For the person who is concerned with the future, the book of Revelation is the timely word of God.

In the course of our years, New Year's Day is a day wherein our concern about the future is expressed. The book of Revelation is the part of Scripture that deals with our concern about the future.

When we begin reading the book of Revelation, we are first confused and then disappointed. We are confused by an author who talks of angels and dragons, men eating books and giant insects eating men, bottomless pits and mysterious numbers, fantastic beasts and golden cities. The language confuses us. And then we are disappointed because we don't find what we are looking for. We want to know what is going to happen in the future, but we find neither dates nor names. We are fearful of what may happen to the world in the next twelve months, but we don't find anything said that helps us understand the coming days. We have some hopes for our lives and for our families, but we find nothing that is said about our prospects. We go back to reading the political analysts and working the horoscope in the paper, escaping occasionally with a science fiction novel and making do as best we can.

So, what has happened? Has the book of Revelation—a holy scripture notwithstanding—failed us? Is the Word of God, though highly regarded in previous centuries, quite inadequate to communicate to our adult, mature world? We put the writer and reader of Revelation in a class with palm readers and fortune tellers—colorful but chancy.

Or is it that we just haven't given it enough thought?

Maybe what is needed is some hard concentration to figure out the symbols, arrange the chronology, and pin down the predictions. Many people have done just that. Obsessed with the future and unwilling to concede that the Bible does not have the final word on it, they twist and arrange the material in it until it finally does yield the word they want to hear. History becomes arranged in prophetic installments. Dates are set and personalities named. The future is known. There is no more uncertainty. But the end result, satisfying as it is, is not recognizable in the book of Revelation.

Maybe this book doesn't need ingenuity as much as open attention. Maybe we have been so obsessed with questions about the future that we haven't heard what Revelation said about it. Maybe we have so fixed in our minds the kind of thing that will be said that we are not able to hear what is actually said. For us, the future means dates, events, and names, and if we do not find them, we either give up in disgust or invent them and put them in anyway. Maybe, though, the future doesn't mean that at all. Maybe God is trying to say something in the book of Revelation that we haven't thought about before that is the truth about the future. Maybe this is a new word—a *really* new word.

This new, unexpected quality is characteristic of

Scripture. Have you noticed how often people question Jesus in the gospel narrative and how regularly his answer ignores their question? Scripture is not an encyclopedia of information to which we go when we are curious or in doubt. It is God speaking to us his own word, telling us what he wishes to tell us and omitting what is of no significance. (Have you ever made a list of all those items you are intensely curious about but for which there is no biblical data?)

The book of Revelation really is about the future, but what it says does not satisfy our curiosity or match what we think are the obvious things to say. It is not a disclosure of future events but the revelation of their inner meaning. It does not tell us what events are going to take place and the dates of their occurrence; it tells us what the meaning of those events is. It does not provide a timetable for history; it gives us an inside look at the reality of history. It is not prediction but perception. It is, in short, about God as he is right now. It rips the veil off our vision and lets us see what is taking place.

The text gives us a summary of what lies behind the veil, behind the newspaper headlines, behind the expressionless mask of a new calendar. Behind all the imaginative caricatures of future events, there is God, who sits on his throne and says, "Behold, I make all things new. . . . I am the Alpha and the Omega, the beginning and the end" (Revelation 21:5–6).

"All things new." Well, we would like that. A new car, maybe a new home, certainly some new clothes. And as long as it is "all things," we may as well expand our list. Some new neighbors, some new weather, a new political climate, a new world peace, a new society of brotherhood. As long as we are wishing, we may as well wish for the works.

But wait a minute. God does not say, "I will make all things new," but said, "I make all things new." It is in the present tense. If he is already doing it, why are so many things old and worn out? Why are we so quickly bored with things? Could it be that we have once again missed the point of the Word of God?

To get back on track, let's look at the way the word *new* was used earlier. Isaiah was a spokesman for the Word of God about four hundred years earlier. There the Word of God was,

Remember not the former things,
    nor consider the things of old.
Behold, I am doing a new thing;
    now it springs forth, do you not perceive it?

I will make a way in the wilderness
    and rivers in the desert.
The wild beasts will honor me,
    the jackals and the ostriches;
for I give water in the wilderness,
    rivers in the desert,
to give drink to my chosen people,
    the people whom I formed for myself
that they might declare my praise. (Isaiah 43:18–21)

That triggers the recollection of another famous instance of the word *new.* This time it is from Saint Paul in 2 Corinthians: "If any one is in Christ, he is a new creation; the old has passed away, behold, the new has come. All this is from God, who through Christ reconciled us to himself and gave us the ministry of reconciliation" (5:17–18).

When God speaks from the throne in Revelation and says, "Behold, I make all things new," he can hardly mean anything very different from what he has already said through Isaiah and Saint Paul. God is with men and women in Christ, meeting them personally, forgiving their sins, and filling them with eternal life. The new is that which God brings to humanity now—the new is now.

In one sense it is not new at all. It is the same new thing that God did at the beginning when he said, "Let there be light" (Genesis 1:3); the same thing as when the Spirit of God came upon King Saul and gave him a new heart (1 Samuel 10:9); the same thing that the crowd around Jesus saw when they exclaimed, "What is this? A new teaching!" (Mark 1:27); and the same thing that Jesus said to Nicodemus: "You must be born anew" (John 3:7). If by *new* we mean the latest fashion, fad, or novel, then this certainly is not new.

> ※ *God is with men and women in Christ,*
> *meeting them personally, forgiving their*
> *sins, and filling them with eternal life.*
> *The new is that which God brings to*
> *humanity now—the new is now.*

On the other hand, if we mean essential life, our encounter with God, the receiving of grace so that our lives can finally be lived without guilt and with steady purpose, then yes, this is the absolutely new. It is that which can never be antiquated. It is that which puts into obsolescence all other experience and knowledge. And as we participate in this new thing, we become a beachhead from which all things are made new. We become the person Saint Paul spoke of—a new creature who has heard the good news and who shares this new report with his or her neighbors.

The statement "I make all things new" is supported by the identification "I am the Alpha and the Omega, the beginning and the end." Alpha is the first letter in the Greek alphabet, and Omega is the last. When translated into our terms, Alpha and Omega comes out as "from A to Z." God's being includes all things. Nothing is excluded from his will and purpose, including time.

It is all God's time. He hasn't reserved only the fifty-two Sundays of the year for his specialized attention. He will not be absent any day or any month. The whole of time is his. There is something more to be said, though, for "the beginning and the end" do not merely mean first and last. A belief in God that is limited to that literalism is too bare. God got things started and he will be around at the finish—most people more or less expect that. But this beginning and end have a more profound meaning. Here, *beginning* means source and origin—the basic substratum underlying all things.

Theologian Paul Tillich has defined God as the "ground of being."* Tillich was trying to get away from

---

* Paul Tillich, *Systematic Theology*, vol. 1 (Chicago: The University of Chicago Press, 1951), 156.

the idea that God is just off in the clouds somewhere or just the first thing that happened in history way back at creation. God is that out of which everything proceeds and exists. God is also the "end" in a more profound sense than that he will be around at the end of the world. The Greek word for "end" (*telos*)* means that he is the destination of all things. His being is the fulfilled purpose for which all things exist.

I can almost hear someone's objection at this point: but I knew all that—I thought Revelation was going to tell me something about the future. All I can answer is, it has. It has taken the same gospel of Jesus Christ—that God is present with us to bring us to new life, to support us, and to fulfill us—and applied it to the future. There is no different gospel for the future than for the present or the past. There is no use casting around for some easier, magical way to live our lives this next year.

On the other hand, the book of Revelation has convinced many people that there is no need to find that impossible, magical view of the future. It helps create room for faith. One theologian wrote, "God guides his

---

* *Strong's*, s.v. "telos" (G5056), Blue Letter Bible, www.blueletterbible.org/lang/lexicon/lexicon.cfm?t=kjv&strongs=g5056.

children around many blind corners. He knows the way they must take. It is the devil who indulges men's desire to see the whole road ahead; he hides only the precipice at the end of the road."*

Every new year, we find a year ahead of us in which God will be making all things new. Of everything that is and of everything that takes place, he will be both the source and the destination. It takes great courage to believe that and great faithfulness to act upon it, for every newspaper in the country will be headlining a contradiction, and your own sin and rebellion will be turning in contrary evidence. All the same, let this word of God tear away the veil that obscures the presence and action of God in the days ahead.

Every day will be a *new* day for God, creation, and redemption. It is only our blindness and sloth that keep us from seeing that openness in it.

As G. K. Chesterton wrote,

Because children have abounding vitality, because they are in spirit fierce and free, therefore they want things repeated and unchanged. They always say, "Do it again"; and the grown-up person

---

* Editor's note: While Eugene attributed this quote to D. T. Niles, the publisher was not able to independently verify its source or wording.

does it again until he is nearly dead. For grown-up people are not strong enough to exult in monotony. But perhaps God is strong enough to exult in monotony. It is possible that God says every morning, "Do it again" to the sun; and every evening, "Do it again" to the moon.*

This wonder brings us back to the throne, where he says, "Behold, I make all things new. . . . I am the Alpha and the Omega, the beginning and the end."

This is the end where we make our beginning.

The end from which we start.

And this end brings us to the beginning of true *thanksgiving*. The art of thanksgiving is to give thanks when you don't feel like it.

It is easy to say thank you when you are filled with a sense of blessedness. It is easy to say thank you when your arms are filled with gifts and you are surrounded by the ones you love; it is, in fact, nearly impossible *not* to say thanks, to sing praises, and to laugh and make merry then.

---

* G. K. Chesterton, *Orthodoxy,* in *Heretics and Orthodoxy* (Bellingham, WA: Lexham, 2017), 220.

A few years ago, on a bright spring Sunday, I met a man I had not seen in years at the entrance to our sanctuary. He had once been an active member of our church but had dropped out years before. I was surprised to see him and said, "Jimmy, what in the world are you doing here? It's great to see you, but how come you chose today?" He said, "I woke up this morning feeling great, and I just had to say thank you. My business is going great, my kids are great, and the day is wonderful. And I had to say thank you to someone— and God seemed the only one adequate to receive all the thanks I am feeling."

And so he did. He worshipped with us that day. He gave thanks. And I haven't seen him since. I understand his wanting to be there that Sunday. But I also understand him not coming back. All of us know how to give thanks on spring Sundays when our kids are beautiful and our work is lovely and the Judas trees are blossoming and the dogwoods are in flower. It is the other times that are difficult.

Giving thanks is one of the most attractive things that we do. Maybe *the* most attractive. There is something whole and robust and generous about the praising person. Even if we cannot give thanks, we like to be around the people who can.

We like it when other people do it. We feel *wonderful* when we ourselves do it. There is a sense of completeness, of mature wholeness. Praise is our best work. A praising life is the best life of all.

It is fitting that Thanksgiving Day is a national holiday for us here in America—the gathering together as friends and families in an act of gratitude, remembering our national origins in acts of thanksgiving. Giving thanks to God in acts like this one, whether of national gratitude or of Christian worship, shows us at our best. We feel it. We aren't just offering our gratitude because our parents told us to do it or out of a vague sense of obligation. We have a deep sense that thankfulness is one of the best things we can do in order to be at *our* best.

There are two books in the Bible that more than any other show the inner life of the person of faith: Psalms and Revelation. Both of them conclude in boisterous acts of praise.

Psalms concludes with five great noisy hallelujah psalms, gathering all that everyone could feel about themselves and God—pain, doubt, despair, joy, rejection, acceptance, the whole bag of human experience—into praise.

Revelation does the same thing. It enters imaginatively into the enormous range of experience that we get ourselves in for when we take the name of Jesus Christ as the definition of our lives, goes through the various depths and heights of dealing with God and the devil, and finally ends up in the same place: praising, singing repeated hallelujahs—in a replay of the Psalms ending. The last hallelujah song is sung as we are ushered into the great hallelujah banquet, the marriage supper of the Lamb that is spread in heaven.

It would seem, on the basis of these accounts, that the way to be a whole person, to live at one's best, would be to live a praising life. To say thank you a lot. To praise God a lot. But this cannot be a superficial thanks. There have, unfortunately, been more than a few people around who have told us to give thanks without first doing the work of honesty. It never seems to make things a whole lot better, does it? A beautiful discipline of the soul can become sappy, mindless counsel, if we divorce it from the biblical roots of honesty, grief, lament, and genuine celebration from which it originates.

No! If we are to live praising lives, robust lives of affirmation, we must live truly, honestly, and courageously. We cannot take shortcuts to the act of praising. We cannot praise prematurely.

> ✳ *If we are to live praising lives, robust*
> *lives of affirmation, we must live truly,*
> *honestly, and courageously. We cannot*
> *take shortcuts to the act of praising. We*
> *cannot praise prematurely.*

Take the psalms, for instance. The psalms, literally *praises,* are not, for the most part, praises at all. They are laments and complaints, angry questions and disappointed meditations. Occasionally there is a good day—the sun shines, no sheep wander off, nobody rips you off—and there is a wonderful song of thanksgiving. But mostly there are laments, complaints, cries of anger, and people fed up with life and wanting God to do something about it—and soon.

Revelation is that way too. There are interludes of heavenly praise: harps and angels and elders throwing their crowns up in the air in jubilation (you can bet that they aren't Presbyterian elders doing that). Yet the story line in Revelation also has to do with trouble: the mess we are in and the seemingly endless difficulties of ever getting out. The cycle happens over and over again—seven times, in fact, until we wonder if it is ever going to come to an end. And then it does: in exuberant rounds of praise, encores of praise, and then the marriage supper—this hallelujah banquet.

It is absolutely essential that we take this pattern and sequence seriously. Premature praise is false praise. Praise is our end but not our beginning. We begin our lives crying, not smiling and cooing and thanking our parents for bringing us into this lovely world full of dry diapers and sweet milk and warm flesh. We kick and flail. We yell and weep.

＊ *We have the popularization of a kind of religion that, instead of training people to the sacrificial life after the pattern of our Lord, seduces them into having fun on weekends.*

We have moments, it is true, when we give praise. But mostly we are aware of wants, of needs, of frustrations, of incompletions. We experience pain and ignorance. We are aware of inadequacy and rejection. In the midst of these poverties, we have moments when everything is wonderful, but that praise is not perpetual. Now, here is the biblical pattern: we don't become praising people by avoiding or skipping or denying the pain and the poverty and the doubt and the guilt but by entering into them, exploring them, minding their significance, embracing the reality of these experiences.

That is what is so distressing about the religious entertainment industry in our land. We have the popularization of a kind of religion that, instead of training people to the sacrificial life after the pattern of our Lord, seduces them into having fun on the weekends, with Jesus as the chief master of ceremonies—much like some sort of talk show host who's here to interview those lucky people who have made it big with God, and the show is interspersed with some upbeat worship music to keep the audience (that's us) from thinking too much about the awful people in the world who are killing and raping and cheating and making such a mess of things that there is really nothing left for them but the Battle of Armageddon.

We, all of us, want to be in a church or some kind of community that serves up the hallelujah banquet every week. Americans seem particularly susceptible to being seduced along these lines. In the nineteenth century, there were several utopian communities that were attempted by high-minded people, not unlike the communes that sprouted during the sixties.

One of the famous ones was Brook Farm in Massachusetts.* It attracted some of the literary luminaries of New England. Among them was Nathaniel Hawthorne. The story of Nathaniel Hawthorne at Brook Farm is reflective of us. Hawthorne was a gloomy man, mostly. He knew the depths of human sin and probed the dark passages of the human condition. But he must have gotten sick of it at one point and wanted out. Brook Farm promised a way out.

At Brook Farm there was no sin. It was conducted on the lines of rational enlightenment. At Brook Farm, people would be living at their best. No stuff of *The Scarlet Letter* or *The House of the Seven Gables* guilt. At Brook Farm, there were only joy and thanksgiving.

But then George Ripley, the guru of Brook Farm, assigned Hawthorne the task of tending the manure pile. And Hawthorne didn't like it and left. He wanted Thanksgiving turkey, not chicken dung. He came to Brook Farm to live with the songs of the angels, not the refuse of the cows and sheep.

---

* For historical context on Brook Farm, see *Encyclopaedia Britannica Online,* s.v. "Brook Farm," www.britannica.com/topic/Brook-Farm.

That's us—wanting the glamour of an idealized life, then growing quickly disillusioned when reality breaks into our daydreams.

The only way genuine, authentic, and deep praise is ever accomplished is by embracing what's real. By accepting whatever takes place and living through it as thoroughly as we are able in faith. For in these moments, in these passages, we become human. We grow up into the fullness of our humanity and into the depths of Christ's salvation that is being worked out among us.

※ *The only way genuine, authentic, and*
deep praise is ever accomplished is by
embracing what's real. By accepting
whatever takes place and living through
it as thoroughly as we are able in faith.
For in these moments, in these passages,
we become human.

Jesus Christ did not arrive at the hallelujah banquet by successfully dodging all the evil in the world, by working out a careful strategy so he could avoid touching every unclean person of his time, and by developing a loyal cadre of friends who would be absolutely true to him through thick and thin. He didn't do that at all.

He went out of his way, it seems, looking for trouble, and when it came, he embraced it. He embraced other people's trouble, but he also embraced his own. He took up the cross. He didn't like it. He didn't thank God for it. He didn't sing a hallelujah hymn in the Garden of Gethsemane. He hated every minute of it. But he *did* it. He *embraced* it. Christ entered the jungle of pain, he explored the wilderness of suffering, and, in the process of the sacrifice, he accomplished redemption. For redemption is not a rescue from evil—it is a redemption of evil. Salvation is not luck but rather a courageous confrontation that is victorious in battle.

And that is why praise is so exhilarating. It has nothing to do with slapping a happy face on a bad situation and grinning through it. It is fashioned deep within us, out of the sin and guilt and doubt and lonely despair that nevertheless *believes*.

And, in that believing, becomes whole.

EPHESUS

I have this against you, that you have
abandoned the love you had at first.
Remember then from what you
have fallen, repent and do
the works you did at first.

—Revelation 2:4–5

The Test of Our Love

Human beings do many extraordinary things. Unlike the animals, we are not content to simply fill our stomachs, find shelter, mate, and frolic a little in the sun on occasion. We humans build splendid buildings. We construct titanic rockets and travel into outer space. We build computers that store and process and interpret information in mind-boggling ways. We train and discipline our bodies to athletic performances that are breathtaking. We paint pictures that penetrate through everyday reality so that the very inside, the true reality in things and people, is laid open. We compose and play music that lifts us out of the humdrum and launches us into ecstasy. We take bodies that are mangled and broken and put them together with surgical procedures. We grow enough food to feed the hungry of the world. We learn about people and cultures far removed from us in space and time and expand our personal worlds so that we are no longer confined and limited by the few decades of trial and error of our life span. And on and on.

※ *When we are living at our best, with all our energies focused, all our abilities alert and involved, doing what we were created to do, we* love.

Our accomplishments are awesome. What do you want to be—athlete, scientist, artist, inventor? What is the best thing you can do with your life? With all the possibilities open and the vast array of examples, you would think that there would be a great deal of argument and confusion about what is best. In fact, there is a surprising consensus—all over the world and all through history. Not absolutely unanimous but very impressive. I think we can say overwhelmingly that the best thing we do is love.

When we are living at our best, with all our energies focused, all our abilities alert and involved, doing what we were created to do, we *love.* Yet there is another aspect to this consensus. That no matter what else we do—no matter if we come home with the Olympic gold or make a million dollars or pioneer the exploration of space or move the world with some artistic performance or discover the cure to cancer—if we do not love, it is not satisfactory.

No matter if we are responsible and work hard and do our jobs well and stay out of trouble and are respected, if we do not *love*, then somehow we have failed. If we live but do not *love*, we miss it.

Notice that I am not reporting on what the Bible says or what Christianity says but what virtually everyone in the history of civilization says. This is the human consensus—*love* is the best thing we do, and it is not a luxury or an option but a necessity if we are to be truly human.

With that quite incredible consensus before us, we are faced with puzzling questions: Why don't we love more? Why aren't we better at it? Why do we settle for so much less? Why do we get diverted and distracted from a life of love? These are the questions that John is putting to his congregations and to us.

John was a pastor to seven churches in the late first century. His congregations were much like our own except that they spoke Greek instead of English, had an emperor in Rome instead of a president in Washington, and wore sandals instead of sneakers. In the essential things they were like us—they got up in the morning and went to bed at night; they ate and drank; they had jobs and lived with families, had good days and bad days, laughed some of the time and cried once in a while.

They were also like us in that they believed in Jesus Christ and experienced themselves as saved—freed from sin and free for God. They met together to grow in that deep and wide life. They sang songs of praise, offered prayers together, encouraged one another. They had heard the good news that God was for them, loved them, was personally interested in them, and had done something radical and final about the mess they kept making of things. As they worshipped, their lives expanded beyond the cramped borders of their egos. When they entered into the praise that pulses at the heart of all existence, they discovered that their quite ordinary lives—that nobody else had thought were good for much—had meaning, and they kept finding meaning in unexpected places. Just like we are doing.

In the middle of all that, some important people got

the idea that these Christians were dangerous. These important people became terribly afraid of their songs and their prayers, and they mounted a campaign to stamp them out. One day Roman soldiers came and took old John away from his churches and put him in exile on the island Patmos. Curious, isn't it, that the soldiers considered the old pastor a threat to their law and order. He had no sword, no army. All he did was teach his people to pray, lead them in worship, teach them songs and Scripture, and train them to live honestly with compassion and fairness.

You might have thought that the government would have been glad to have these little pockets of cheerful and morally sane people scattered through the society, but they weren't. They were scared to death of them. They sensed, correctly enough as it turned out, that singing those songs and studying those scriptures and believing in Jesus Christ would completely revolutionize the world and in not very many years leave the Roman military and political giant crippled and ineffectual. So, they arrested John and put him in exile, hoping that his congregations would wither away.

One Sunday John was praying and received a vision

of Jesus Christ doing his work of love and salvation in the midst of all this angry, fearful hostility. He wrote down what he saw and heard and then smuggled it onto the mainland. The scroll got into the right hands. The word was passed. The Christians met cautiously and secretly. When everyone was assembled, one would read from the scroll what their old pastor had written down for them, the vision that gave them vision to see the world as it really was.

It is as if John's saying to his beloved congregation: "Do you think that Rome is running things? It is not. *Christ* is running things, and this is how he is doing it. Do you think that persecution and blasphemy and death and Caesar are the last words? They are not. Worship and life and praise and the living Christ are the last words."

After the scroll was read in one congregation, it was passed surreptitiously to the next, until all seven had read it. The people were convinced by it that their lives counted, that everything they did was critically significant in what Christ was doing in redeeming the world. They became steadfast. Cheerful. Bold.

What stirring times those were! Real persecution heightened the importance of what they were doing and sharpened all their senses. Roman persecution, in an unintended way, convinced the Christians beyond wavering that they were on the right track. If the government was aroused over a few lower-class people saying their prayers and confessing their Christ, then prayer and confessing Christ must be highly significant acts. The scroll was passed from church to church. Early in the scroll were individualized messages to each of the seven churches; each congregation's uniqueness was recognized and addressed. These are the messages we are looking at, one by one, submitting ourselves to examination: the final exams that show us where we are in relation to Christ's great presence among us and his great work among us.

Saint John's letters to his seven congregations subjected each church to an individual examination. Saint John said that Christ, the light of the world, is standing in our midst. Christ's brilliance shows us just what we are—it probes into all the dark places in our lives and brings everything into the daylight. The light of our Lord first provides a diagnosis, but after it provides the diagnosis, it becomes a healing presence. A medicine is prescribed for each. "The light shines in the darkness, and the darkness has not overcome it" (John 1:5).

Christians have not changed so much in twenty centuries. The Christian life is still lived in human lives that are subject to eternal questions. Christ is in our church. He examines our lives to bring us out into the open, where we can live freely as forgiven persons without guilt or regret. Let us submit to the examination. Let us allow the light of Christ to probe our lives, expose our failings, and heal our sickness.

＊ *Christ's brilliance shows us just what we are—it probes into all the dark places in our lives and brings everything into the daylight.*

Again, each of the letters follows a similar outline: First, Christ *presents* a particular part of his character. Next, Christ *examines* the Christians. The examination reveals both strengths and weaknesses, and so corrective action is commanded. Then, an urgent *promise* concludes each message.

To the Christians at Ephesus: "I have this against you, that you have abandoned the love you had at first. Remember then from what you have fallen, repent and do the works you did at first" (Revelation 2:4–5). The examination revealed some great things about the

Ephesian Christians. They were hard workers. They didn't give up easily. They were faced with constant opposition, but they didn't waver. There were daily acts of mercy and compassion to perform, and they did them with regularity. They didn't forget to gather together, despite the danger, to worship each Lord's Day. They were also discerning about doctrine.

Some heretics, the Nicolaitans, were trying to worm themselves into the church and upset its devotion to Christ. They were a group that denied the necessity for any moral standards—they taught that you could love Christ and do what you liked. But the Ephesians were not taken in by the attractiveness of the doctrine—while they bore up under the persecutions and adversities very well, they did not tolerate these evil men. They were a vigorous, alert group of Christians. Christ commended them for all this—he knew it well and approved of it. But he also saw something else. In their vigor to do the right thing, they had become the wrong kind of people. What more could you ask of Christians? Well, love for one thing. "I have this against you, that you have abandoned the love you had at first" (verse 4).

Love was the beginning of their faith. And ours too, of course. The foundation of Christianity is an immense act of love—the love of God for them, for us, for all who come to God. For them, it was the beginning of a new life. God's love for them was the experience that brought everything else to *wholeness*. Their love for God involved them in a life that had purpose, intensity, and passion. Their love for one another diversified and extended the experience. As they went along, though, they found it easier to keep doing everything else but love. Their pastor was blunt: "Remember then from what you have fallen" (verse 5). This was not a gentle drifting away but rather a catastrophic fall. This was not an item that they happened to overlook in the press of urgent concerns. This fall was so massive in its implications that they might as well have been leaving the center of existence. For love is not what we do after we get the other things done, if we have any energy left over. Love is what we do, period. It is not how we work; it is our work. Other things can support it, they can grow out of it, and they can lead up to it. But if we don't love, we aren't doing what we were created and saved to do.

Why did the Ephesians abandon their first love, the love of God—the primary love, the essential love? Why did they go on to fritter their lives away in all these good but lesser things? Because everything else was easier. None of it was bad or harmful as such, and most of it had to be done, sometime or another. They weren't hurting anybody, and they were helping many. But they weren't at their best. They were not living at that center where the action of God is in full force. In a word, they were lazy. They were working day and night, doing good deeds, teaching the truth, opposing falsehood, impressing themselves and one another with their industriousness—all because they were too lazy to love.

Love is not what we do after we get the other things done, if we have any energy left over. Love is what we do, period.

Ephesus had the reputation of being the love capital of the ancient world. The fertility love goddess, Artemis, had a great shrine in Ephesus. The goddess with a thousand breasts attracted the curiosity of tourists and the devotion of the unloved looking for love. She was famous and impressive and popular. There was only one thing wrong: it wasn't love; it was lust. It was the manipulation of appetite and the exploitation of bodies. Artemis was false advertising. Love packaged as a commodity was the biggest business in Ephesus.

Human desire was bought and sold for profit. Men

and women reaching for and longing after the best they could be were tricked into squalor. Healthy sexuality was debased into sordid pornography. But in this very city, there were some people who were onto the real thing: Love that gave. Love that accepted. Love that was sacrificial and redemptive. Love that paid its promises. Love that wasn't out to get but out to give. Love that didn't leave you wasted and cheapened but fulfilled and enriched. Love that brought the longings for more, for excellence, for passion, and for wholeness into all affairs of everyday life.

Then, like Hawthorne at Brook Farm, the Christians in Ephesus quit. They quit because it was too much for them. It demanded their total selves. It required them to keep their whole being in Christ. It didn't seem like such a bad thing to quit; after all, there were plenty of important church jobs to do, and there was a moral life to lead, and there was all that evil in the city to fight against. Then they got John's letter, his vision, and the line addressed just to them, which I'll paraphrase:

I know all the good things you are doing, but I have this against you: you are a bunch of quitters! You abandoned the first love, the very first thing that you were called to experience and share. And in Ephesus of all places—where so many people are looking for the real thing and being sold a bunch of fraudulent substitutes. And do you know something? Listen now closely: I really don't need any more church jobs done, any more morality exhibited, any more evil fought. What I need is some people who will do the central, the essential, the Christian thing. I need people who will love—love Christ, be loved by Christ, love your neighbors, be loved by your neighbors.

Love is what Christ still requires of us. It is what he won't do without. If we won't do it, he will go on and find someone who will. He is not going to lower himself to our standards. Instead, he is going to raise us to his: *to love.* In the end, we will be judged on our love. "I have this against you, that you have abandoned the love you had at first." Terrible words! The God who is for us is against us! But he wouldn't be for us if he let us get by living without love, would he?

The Ephesians' strongest virtue became the source of their failing—they worked so hard to be right and correct that they forgot who they were being good to and how their righteousness affected others: "You have abandoned the love you had at first." You have lost your first love. Saint Paul wrote the following to a group of Christians in Corinth who had a similar problem:

> If I speak in the tongues of men and of angels, but have not love, I am a noisy gong or a clanging cymbal. And if I have prophetic powers, and understand all mysteries and all knowledge, and if I have all faith, so as to remove mountains, but have not love, I am nothing. If I give away all I have, and if I deliver my body to be burned, but have not love, I gain nothing. (1 Corinthians 13:1–3)

Back in the early days of their Christian life, the Ephesians had been enthusiastic in love. They were one of the groups that the pagans looked at and exclaimed, "How they love one another!" There was a transforming energy that was at work in them. They reconciled enemies, they helped the poor and sick, they worshipped with joy—and all their work was brimming with love for their Lord and for their brothers and sisters.

Jeremiah preached to Israel in the sixth century BC—Israel, who also was vigorous in doing things but had forgotten about love:

> I remember the devotion of your youth,
>> your love as a bride,
> how you followed me in the wilderness,
>> in a land not sown. (Jeremiah 2:2)

Back in the beginning there was a love affair, remember? Back in those early days, life was dominated by the thought of the God who loved us and gave himself for us. Back in the beginning it was like a honeymoon, a courtship. Remember?

Our Lord examined the Ephesian Christians and had this—abandoning love—against them. He examines us and has the same thing against us. But he didn't only diagnose. He also prescribed a cure: "Remember then from what you have fallen, repent and do the works you did at first. If not, I will come to you and remove your lampstand from its place, unless you repent" (Revelation 2:5). Remember, repent, and go back to work like when you started out.

The remembrance is useless if it moves into indifference or rebellion. Repentance is the resolve to return to those early truths, the first reality, that we felt really secure upon. The days of our history may rust and corrode the best realities of our lives, and we need to get cleaned up once in a while. Some changes have to be made. We have to return to what Christ first meant to us.

The important thing right now is not whether you pass the test but that you *take* the test. By taking it, we acknowledge that it is this by which we want to be judged. By taking it, we grasp the God of love openly, receiving him and sharing him as if nothing else in the whole world matters, for in truth nothing else does.

The examination concluded with an urgent promise: "He who has an ear, let him hear what the Spirit says to the churches. To him who conquers I will grant to eat of the tree of life, which is in the paradise of God" (Revelation 2:7).

The promise wasn't given casually. It wasn't offered as a pleasant option. There was urgency, necessity, in it. He who has an ear, *hear.* Henry Ward Beecher once said, "The Churches of the land are sprinkled all over with baldheaded old sinners whose hair has been worn off by the constant friction of countless sermons that have been aimed at them and glanced off and hit the man in the pew behind."*

The promise is that the Christian who recaptures that first love—the one who becomes what he was called to be by Christ—will eat of the tree of life in God's paradise. That brings us back to Genesis and the garden with the tree of life, the garden from which Adam and Eve were expelled and the tree of life from which no one ever ate. The tree of life bears fruit that enables us to live eternally with God. It is the food that finally satisfies our needs. By returning to the first love, we are rewarded with the first food. The return to our origin includes a return to God, who not only loves us but feeds us. When we return to loving God and the world for which he died, we return to Eden.

❋ *When we return to loving God and the world for which he died, we return to Eden.*

Examine yourselves. Have you strayed from your first love of Christ and those early bursts of love for

---

* Henry Ward Beecher, quoted in William Barclay, *Letters to the Seven Churches* (Louisville, KY: Westminster John Knox, 2001), 14.

your neighbors? Are you truly loving your brothers and sisters? Remember, repent, and then do the works you did at first—*love.*

Do this in remembrance of Christ.

Amen.

SMYRNA

Do not fear what you are about to
suffer. . . . Be faithful unto death, and
I will give you the crown of life.

—Revelation 2:10

The Test of Our Suffering

After about an hour and a half of driving on our way to the ocean in the summer—a trip we make once or twice a year—just when it is getting hot and we are getting bored, we enter the town of Smyrna, Delaware. The name, like the ring of an alarm clock, wakes me up. Then, over on the right is the church of St. Polycarp. Another clang. The two names activate engrams in my brain cells that keep me alert the rest of the way to the beach.

It is dangerous to drive the highways of America. If you want to preserve your life, keeping secure and cozy, stay off the highways, where you not only have to dodge drunk drivers, who might at any moment murderously swerve into you, but also have to avoid all the towns that set stories going in your mind that demand you give up your life. People who quit reading the Bible ages ago and haven't been to church in years drive through Nazareth, Bethlehem, Bethesda, Joppa, and Damascus, and before they know it, Jesus, who said, "Deny yourself and take up your cross daily," and Paul, who said, "I am crucified with Christ," are saying it again* as old memories resonate. We drive through Ephrata, Bethany, and Philadelphia—and Smyrna—and are ambushed by a gospel story.

Part of the reason that going through these towns has made such an impact on me is that I didn't grow up around names like them. Like for all children, names were important to me. I grew up in Montana and Washington, and when I was young, my family would travel those roads and I would hear the names of the towns—Missoula, Kila, Kootenai, Pocatello, Issaquah, Puyallup, Sequim, Yakima, Walla Walla—wonderful names, Indian names most of them, names that evoked the wilderness that one encountered nowhere else. And in the midst of all that strangeness there was Libby. *Libby?* Some logger's girlfriend, maybe, some trapper's woman who left him. My childish mind fantasized scenarios of those. And not far from there was Eureka, an

---

* These are paraphrases of Luke 9:23 and Galatians 2:20.

unexpected evidence of culture. Eureka was the Greek exclamation "I have found it!" *What on earth did anyone find in that place?* I sometimes wondered. *What was worth exclaiming over, tucked way back into a range of mountains?*

When I left the West and came to the East, one of the things that surprised me was the names of towns: names that I had read about, names like Bethlehem, Nazareth, Salem, Bethel, Joppa, Hebron, Emmaus, Ephrata, Bethany, Bethesda. All up and down this coast, there are towns that were named from another map: the map of faith. The people who traveled along these plains and valleys were not Indians or trappers or loggers. These people were pilgrims. They were disciples following their Lord, and there was something about their journey that was more like that of the people of faith two and three thousand years ago. And it was different from the geography that was thousands of miles away. I loved it when I drove into Bethlehem or into Philadelphia or Bethesda or Goshen or Joppa. We were a long way from the biblical geography, but we were still inside the biblical experience.

But *Smyrna*. What is Smyrna doing in Delaware, interrupting my escape to the beach? Smyrna is where Christians suffered and went to their death rather than deny Christ. Their pastor, John, put steel in their wills with his great vision: "Do not fear what you are about to suffer. . . . Be faithful unto death, and I will give you the crown of life" (Revelation 2:10). They didn't fear. They did die. And they received the crown of life.

One of those martyrs was Polycarp. Why did this American congregation name its church *Polycarp?* Polycarp is not mentioned in the biblical text. He was about thirty years old when John wrote his message. More than fifty years later, he was the pastor in the same church, when another wave of persecution rolled in. Just as John had been arrested earlier, Polycarp was also arrested. (Remember, Polycarp had been among those whom John had addressed in this message to their church! These words from his pastor, John, had encouraged him.)

Polycarp was taken to an arena where great crowds gathered to see Christians burned. It was like the NFL; it drew the same sort of crowds (and probably for some of the same reasons) that football teams draw today.

The proconsul set Polycarp in the middle of the field, confronted him, and said, "Curse Christ."

He replied, "Eighty-six years I have served him, and

he never did me any wrong. How can I blaspheme my King who saved me?"

The proconsul persisted. "Swear by the fortune of Caesar."

Polycarp answered, "You do not know who I am . . . : I am a Christian."

The proconsul roared, "I have wild beasts. I shall throw you to them, if you do not change your mind."

Polycarp said, "Call them. For repentance from the better to the worse is not permitted to us; but it is noble to change from what is evil to what is righteous."

The proconsul said, "I shall have you consumed with fire, if you despise the wild beasts."

Polycarp replied, "The fire you threaten burns but an hour and is quenched after a little. . . . Why do you delay? Come, do what you will."*

Polycarp stood serenely defiant. The killing flames were lit. And Polycarp burned while the world watched.

I soon find myself miles down the road, my imagination spinning with Smyrna and Polycarp. The stories administer the martyr test to me: Who are my heroes?

---

* See Massey Hamilton Shepherd Jr., trans. and ed., "The Martyrdom of Polycarp," in *Early Christian Fathers*, ed. Cyril C. Richardson et al. (New York: Touchstone, 1996), 152–53.

The self-indulgent or the self-sacrificing? Am I willing to embrace suffering? Am I faithful to Christ, dying the little deaths of ego, or am I holding on for dear life to myself?

 Am I faithful to Christ, dying the little deaths of ego, or am I holding on for dear life to myself?

Suddenly we are at Rehoboth Beach. Another gospel name! Abraham and Sarah's son, Isaac, met suffering after suffering, loss after loss in the valley of Gerar. He dug a well and it was taken from him. Then another and he lost that. He persisted faithfully. He dug a third well and, unexpectedly, found himself on the other side of the trouble. He named it Rehoboth ("roomy place," is how I'd translate it), a deep well in a wide place. But it was only through giving up what he thought was his life that he got there. We don't get the Christ-life without the self-death. There is no road to Easter except through Lent. The only way to Rehoboth is through Smyrna.

There were seven churches in all to whom John was their pastor, and the scroll vision was passed to all of them. This was done to encourage them and convince them that their confession and loyalty to Jesus Christ were in fact a revolutionary act that was part of the transformation of all reality from violent, bestial destruction to powerful life-loving creation. Inserted into the vision were seven individualized messages to the seven church congregations. Ephesus got a warning: "You have abandoned your first love." Smyrna got a promise (I paraphrase, of course): "Things are going to get worse. You are going to suffer even more than you are right now. Don't give in. Be faithful unto death, and I will give you the crown of life."

Why did a group of people in Delaware three hundred years or so ago name their village Smyrna? I wonder. Was it a dangerous time? Were they tempted to unfaithfulness? Possibly under pressure to abandon their Christian way of life for something less demanding? Did they name their town Smyrna as a way of identifying with people who were willing to go to their death rather than retract one bit from their Lord, who had gone to his death for them?

You can be sure that the words of his old pastor, John, were still audible to Polycarp as he died—the words of the first and the last, who died and came to life: "I know your tribulation. . . . Do not fear what you are about to suffer. . . . Be faithful unto death, and I will give you the crown of life" (Revelation 2:9–10). And a group of early American Christians named their church for Polycarp. But why? Perhaps to keep before them the example of the person who was faithful to death and fearless in the face of opposition. To remind them that the sequence is not life to death but death to life.

Every time that I have driven Route 13 and slowed down to go through the town of Smyrna and seen the sign of the church of St. Polycarp, I have been on my way to the beach—to enjoy myself, to have a few hours without any pressure from anybody, to luxuriate in the sun. I am aware of the contrast with those who are stuck in poverty, who are plunged into immense suffering, who are faced with hard questions such as, Will I forsake my faith in order to live on the terms that the world gives, or will I forsake life on the world's terms in order to die for Christ? I live in a culture and a society where hardly anyone knows the meaning of the word *sacrifice,* where suffering is something to be avoided at all costs and complained of when it can't be avoided, and where it is unthinkable that there is anything more important than preserving and extending my life.

For three hundred years of the church's life, the single most important model of the Christian life was that of a martyr—the person whose witness was authentic to the point of death. In a society where there were rather frequent instances when faith involved conflict to the point of death, martyrdom became the model. By contrast, the distance between that time and ours can be measured by the difference in our models: the athlete, the millionaire, the entertainer—all persons who are displaying various approaches by their performance and way of life to convince us that death is remote. The athlete in her use of her body, the millionaire in his power to command ease and pleasure, the entertainer by banishing gloomy thoughts and pessimistic attitudes.

※ *For three hundred years of the church's life, the single most important model of the Christian life was that of a martyr— the person whose witness was authentic to the point of death.*

But for a long time, the model was a *martyr*. And for some Christians it still is. Are you willing to die for your faith? And are you willing to give up anything along the way in order to pursue it—those little deaths that sometimes seem as difficult as the final one, dying to impulses of ambition, of lust, of pride, of security, of comfort?

※ *If we spend all our energies trying to protect our interests, to preserve our safety, and to negotiate and compromise with the opposition in order to keep what we have at all costs, we will live meagerly. But if we live at risk, giving up all in witness and commitment and love, we are released from death to live in the power of the Resurrection.*

Here we have one of those paradoxes that are strewn all through the Christian's life of faith. Until we pass the martyr test, we live neither deeply nor widely. Until we are ready to die for Christ, we can't live for him freely, openly, and exuberantly. If we spend all our energies trying to protect our interests, to preserve our safety, and to negotiate and compromise with the opposition in order to keep what we have at all costs, we will live meagerly. But if we live at risk, giving up all in witness and commitment and love, we are released from death to live in the power of the Resurrection.

I've asked myself these questions many times: What is the best thing to say to a person who is suffering? What is the *true* thing to say? What can one say to the person in pain? There is always some embarrassment in saying anything. After all, I am not suffering. I am not having to undergo the trial of faith, of sense, of meaning. Isn't there something presumptuous, an element of arrogance, in saying anything at all? For the person can always respond, "It is well enough for you to talk like that, but it is not you who is suffering." Plus, there is equal danger in saying the wrong thing. What if what you say gives false hope and its consequences are a deeper disillusionment? What if what you say misses the point so completely that you do not help but hinder?

The second church given a personal word of counsel in Saint John's revelation of Jesus Christ was a church that was suffering. And as a pastor with the deepest of concerns for their pain, John spoke a true word of God to them. He began by saying that Christ had a personal word to speak to them and then described this Christ as "the first and the last, who died and came to life" (Revelation 2:8). To describe Christ as "the first and the last" is to say that he includes everything within himself. He is at the beginning and at the end; all that occurs between occurs in the context of his presence. He doesn't appear on the scene when the play is half over, nor does he leave before the final curtain. He is the first and the last. That is a pretty important word to say to a church that is suffering. Christ is at the beginning. We did not get started in life without his presence. Whatever our state now, we didn't get here by ourselves or without God. And Christ is here until the finish. However bereft we seem to be of his presence in our pain, he has not gone off and left us. Existence does not occur outside the confines of Christ's first and last. We are hemmed in by his grace.

The phrase Saint John used parallel to "the first and the last" is startling: "who died and came to life." That is just the reverse of what we use to describe people we know. We say "who was born and died." We think of life as the beginning and death as the end. And the terror of suffering is that it threatens to bring the end closer. But Christ was described in opposite terms: "who died and came to life." Death is for him the beginning. Instead of disaster, it became resurrection. And it is this person—this person who suffered as we suffer, who felt pain as deeply as we will ever feel pain, who endured anguish, doubt, and fear, and who finally felt even death—who takes death as the beginning point and speaks living words of life.

With such a Christ speaking to us, we cannot resent his words as if they were words spoken safely and remotely—words of some healthy, cheerful person to a suffering, depressed person. Christ has felt all that we will feel. And we cannot dismiss his words as being mistaken simply because they do not fully encompass either all that came before or all that might come in the future. No, *Christ is the first and the last*. He knows the preceding days, and he will be present in the impending ones. It is such a person who speaks to the suffering person. Christ has authority to speak because he has been through it all himself, one with something true to say because there is no aspect of suffering, even death itself, that he has not examined in his own life. It is this Christ who examined his Christians in the city of Smyrna. He said, "I know your tribulation and your poverty (but you are rich) and the slander of those who say that they are Jews and are not, but are a synagogue of Satan" (verse 9).

We can partially reconstruct from these words the nature of the suffering of the Smyrnaean Christians. They had tribulation. The word means, literally, "pressure."* The term came from the society in which they lived. Society was pagan in spirit and Roman in government. The pressure came from a law that combined the two elements—that insisted all members of society prove their allegiance by worshipping the emperor. It was not a bad law from the point of view of those who made it. Rome had to unify a vast empire of diverse peoples, who had their own languages, customs, religions, and habits of life. The government sought a point of unity in the emperor. He was proclaimed as God, and everyone's allegiance was tested by their willingness to worship him as such. It was a liberal policy, as everyone could do as they pleased in every area of life if they would come to the government shrine, offer a simple sacrifice, and proclaim in public, "Caesar is Lord." After that they could worship whatever other gods they wished, engage in whatever trade they wanted, speak whatever language they had been taught.

But the Christians would not do it. They said, "Christ is Lord," and would not compromise their wit-

* *Strong's*, s.v. "thlipsis" (G2347), Blue Letter Bible, www.blueletterbible.org /lang/lexicon/lexicon.cfm?t=kjv&strongs=g2347.

ness to give Caesar even half a place. The pressures mounted. Suspicion increased. Persecutions were instigated. The Christians lived under constant intense harassment. Anxiety became pervasive.

And the economic results for Christians was poverty. Because they would not play by the rules, they were excluded from the game. The Christians found it difficult to sell as merchants, to buy as consumers, and to get employed as workers. They were suspect because they would not do what the rest were doing. They were separated from the business and working community because everyone believed they were not quite trustworthy. And so they were poor.

Added to that was the "slander of those who say that they are Jews." The Christians might have thought they would have allies in the Jews, who had suffered so much for their faith through the centuries. But they did not get allies. They got the opposite. They were cursed instead. Much of the slander came from a theological interpretation of their plight.

There was an old strain of thinking among the Jews—we see traces of it in the Old Testament—that equated prosperity with righteousness. If you were good, you were rich. If you did the right thing, you got the rewards of long life and health and luxury. On the other hand, if you were bad, you were punished with poverty and sickness. The Jews looked at the Christians—poor, persecuted, suffering—and came to their heretical conclusion: "You Christians are in the bad shape you are because God is punishing you." That would have been the hardest blow of all. You can take a lot of suffering if you are doing it for the right reason. But if others should say that it is all in vain, that you have put up with all this out of a mistaken notion, that would take the heart out of you.

※ *Jesus, in effect, says to the suffering, "I*
   know. I know everything that is taking
   place. I know from my own experience,
   and I know because I am with you in
   your experience."

To all this, Christ said (I paraphrase, of course), "I know. I know your tribulation, your poverty, the slander of the Jews." Christ was aware of all that they were going through. One of the worst effects of suffering is the sense of isolation that it brings. We feel that in our pain we are cut off from God and from all friends. A friend recently described to me his feelings when he was returning from a bombing mission in Austria in World War II to his base in North Africa. He developed engine trouble and started to go into the Mediterranean. He was sure he was going to die. He didn't have any of the classic reactions or see his life flash before him. He had only one thought: *I'm dying and nobody knows it. Nobody knows I'm going in. Nobody will ever know what happened. Nobody knows.*

Jesus, in effect, says to the suffering, "I know. I know everything that is taking place. I know from my own experience, and I know because I am with you in your experience. I suffered. I died. I know your suffering and your death." When someone is sick or suffering and we say to her that we are thinking of her and praying for her, we are reflecting and sharing in this "I know" of our Lord. When we send flowers, cards, and letters and make visits to her, we are the people in whom Christ lives and who are evidences of his presence, signs of our Lord's knowing. Ours is partial and fragmentary, of course. But it is a reminder of that complete knowledge that our Lord has of our pain and our impending death. We are not isolated. We are not separated either from God or from his people. He knows, and he is with us.

The examination remedied the deepest kind of suffering in the Christians in Smyrna. Next, Christ spoke his word of correction and prescribed help: "Do not fear what you are about to suffer. Behold, the devil is about to throw some of you into prison, that you may be tested, and for ten days you will have tribulation. Be faithful unto death, and I will give you the crown of life" (Revelation 2:10).

"Do not fear." Isn't fear a major part of suffering? Fear of the unknown, fear of isolation, fear of death? But Christ is with us. Do not fear.

One psalmist wrote, "When I am afraid, I put my trust in thee" (Psalm 56:3). I recall hearing a story once about a man who kept tabs on his fears. He discovered that a third of them never materialized. Another third were beyond his control; he couldn't do a thing about them no matter how much he fretted. And the final third were worth worrying about because they were within his control. The false fears he could forget, and by taking thought, he could resolve some of the others and prepare himself to face the rest. The ratio seems about right to me.

"For ten days you will have tribulation." That

sounds cryptic but is quite simple. "Ten days" was a common Greek expression for a brief time. Our counterpart is "a couple of days," "three or four days," or "a day or so." Christ does not say we will not have tribulation and suffering. He does say that it will come to an end. It is limited; it is not interminable eternity.

"Be faithful unto death." Trusting in our Lord and worshipping him are what we are called upon to maintain. Suffering has an end because Christ suffered, died, and lives again. Our sufferings are made endurable because we have one who suffered for us and shares his life with us while we suffer. "Be faithful unto death" in that context is not an unreasonable call to stoicism or just to grit our teeth and carry on; it is a promise of a companion and a presence.

Finally, there is the urgent promise: "I will give you the crown of life. . . . He who conquers shall not be hurt by the second death" (verses 10–11). There are two words in the Greek language for "crown." One is the crown that a king wears, while the other is the prize given to an athlete after winning a race or an honor bestowed on someone by the community for valorous service. This second word is used here. When we participate in sufferings, we are competing in a contest for faith. And when we finish the contest praising God, we are crowned with the prize of life.

The second death referred to, the death that will not touch the conqueror, is the death that separates us from God. The first death that we all have to meet, as Saint Paul once wrote, cannot separate us from the love of Christ. And those who maintain their faith through suffering will never suffer the pangs of separation from God. We will suffer the pain of separation from health, from friends, from children, and from this beautiful world, but we will never be separated from God.

There can be no question about it. The words of the first and the last, the one who died and who lives, who said, "I know your sufferings," and who said, "Do not fear. . . . Be faithful unto death. . . . I will give you the crown of life. . . . He who conquers shall not be hurt by the second death"—those words gave strength and eternity to the lives of Polycarp and the suffering Christians of Smyrna. And they have the power to give strength and eternity to our lives too.

Amen.

PERGAMUM

I have a few things against you:
you have some there who hold
the teaching of Balaam.

—Revelation 2:14

The Test of Our Truth

We live in an odd time. The age we live in has word making as one of the biggest businesses going. Schools and computers, between them, account for most of what is going on today. Schools teach us how to recognize and put words together; computers store and process and retrieve words. Words. There was a time when words were what people used to pass an afternoon around a potbellied stove in the general store, to write a sonnet to a lady, or to request a second helping of potatoes and pork chops. Words were used, but they were not organized. Words were part of the human condition, but nobody made a business out of them. Now words are big business.

With this great emphasis on words, you might think

they are studied and valued and understood more than ever before. But that is where the odd thing appears. They are not. They are used badly, sloppily, carelessly. They are wasted away. It turns out that words themselves are not nearly as important as what they can do, and when they have done their work, they are tossed aside like Kleenex. Words are used in order to influence, to sell a car or a candidate, to seduce, to persuade, to win for propaganda or for advertisement. The skill of our times is not using words as words but using them as weapons, as tools.

※ *One of the large and persistent tasks of living the Christian life is learning to tell the truth.*

One of the large and persistent tasks of living the Christian life is learning to tell the truth. The opposite of telling the truth is telling lies. We lie a lot. Most of us lie a lot. We lie a lot more than we are aware of. We lie even when we think we are telling the truth. The reason we do so is quite clear: we want to be at the center of the action; we want to subordinate all reality, persons, things, and events to our willfulness. We want to control people's responses and manipulate their perceptions. In order to do that, we arrange the data, filter the facts, and shape the information so that we can influence the way things will be heard and seen, so that the response will be congenial to us.

Lies are not usually blatant falsehoods. In order to be successful, they have to be *mostly* truth.

※ *Lies are not usually blatant falsehoods. In order to be successful, they have to be* mostly *truth.*

Lying is a product not so much of maliciousness but of laziness. Most people tell lies with the best of intentions. They think that they are helping the cause of their country or company or their own fortunes and that this is the best way. Few people, at least at the outset, have bad motives or evil intent. They simply want something good or attractive or pleasing to take place, and the lie seems a shortcut to make it happen. Lying seems easier than the truth. Most people don't have the patience to go into all the ramifications of the truth. So, they lie.

The words of him who has the sharp two-edged sword.... Some there who hold the teaching of Balaam. (Revelation 2:12, 14)

When Saint John introduces the letter to the Christians in Pergamum by describing Christ as having a sharp sword proceeding from his mouth, we know that he is going to have something decisive to say. We are about to hear words that are going to make a difference.

In the letter to the Hebrews, we are told,

> The word of God is living and active, sharper than any two-edged sword, piercing to the division of soul and spirit, of joints and marrow, and discerning the thoughts and intentions of the heart. And before him no creature is hidden, but all are open and laid bare to the eyes of him with whom we have to do. (Hebrews 4:12–13)

Because Christ is introduced this way, we assume that the Pergamene Christians had become sloppy with their words. Their way of talking about their faith had become fuzzy. Whatever else they were doing, their speech about their faith needed sharpening. This Christ, with the sword proceeding from his mouth, examined his Christians, and the first thing he said was highly commendatory: "I know where you are living, where Satan's throne is. Yet you are holding fast to my name, and you did not deny your faith in me even in the days of Antipas my witness, my faithful one, who was killed among you, where Satan lives" (Revelation 2:13, NRSV).

These people had lived through difficult times. Their city had seen a furious assault on all who had been brave enough to be Christians. Emperor worship, which was so fiercely intolerant of any who refused to participate in it, had victims from the Pergamene congregation. When the decree came to renounce Christ and worship Caesar, these Christians had shown their true colors and had been brave and stalwart.

There was one famous martyr among them—Antipas was his name. He had died rather than renounce his faith in Christ. And apparently, from the way the commendation is worded, he hadn't been alone. He had the support and allegiance of all the Christians there. This was a heroic church, and it had the bones of martyrs to prove it.

To live in Pergamum was dangerous. Christ said he knew it was; he knew they lived in perhaps the most dangerous spot in the empire. There is a great truth here.

When the New Testament speaks of the Christian dwelling anywhere in this world, it ordinarily uses the Greek word *paroikein*. . . . the word which describes a *temporary* residence in contrast with a permanent residence. . . . The word *paroikein* looks on the Christian as a stranger and a pilgrim. . . . But the significant thing about this passage is that it is not the word *paroikein* which is used; it is *katoikein;* and *katoikein* is the word that is regularly used for *residence in a permanent and settled place.* What the Risen Christ is saying to the Christians in Pergamos is this: "You are living in a city where the influence and the power of Satan are rampant—*and you have to go on living there.* . . . In Pergamos you are, and in Pergamos you must stay. Life has set you where Satan's seat is. It is *there* you must live; and it is *there* you must show that you are a Christian." . . .

It is no part of the Christian duty to run away from a difficult and a dangerous situation. The Christian aim is not escape from a situation, but conquest of a situation.*

---

* William Barclay, *Letters to the Seven Churches* (Louisville, KY: Westminster John Knox, 2001), 35–36.

But despite their valor under the most extreme persecution, Christ had something more to say: "I have a
few things against you: you have some there who hold
the teaching of Balaam, who taught Balak to put a
stumbling block before the sons of Israel, that they
might eat food sacrificed to idols and practice immorality" (verse 14).

✳ *As we realize how vast the resources*
and energy of God are in our everyday
lives, we find that we don't have to carry
the weight of the world's sins on our
shoulders, that our moral sweat isn't
going to make the critical difference in
history, but that the difference has al-
ready been made by Christ's blood.

I've noticed that people who read the Bible tend to
laugh a lot. There are comic passages in this book that
double us up with laughter. But the laughter is more
than entertainment. It teaches us, too. There are some
insights we get only while laughing. The story of
Balaam is one of these comic passages. Solemnity is not
a mark of religious depth. It is not true, as many people

seem to assume, that the more serious we get about God, the more serious we get. Often the opposite takes place: we get serious about God and get lighthearted about everything else.

Maturing in our life of faith brings us to a sense of God's grace. As we realize how vast the resources and energy of God are in our everyday lives, we find that we don't have to carry the weight of the world's sins on our shoulders, that our moral sweat isn't going to make the critical difference in history, but that the difference has already been made by Christ's blood.

And so, not infrequently, we come to stories in Scripture that provide a kind of comic relief: we see the ridiculousness of pretention in human effort, how funny it is when people think they are doing the work of God or are trying to act like gods. It is like little kids dressing up in their parents' clothes—they are deadly serious about it, pretending to be adults. But to us look-ing on, it is funny. They look so silly strutting around in shoes too big for them, in hats that fall down over their ears, and in coats and dresses that drag on the ground and trip them up as they walk. That is the kind of story we have with Balaam.

The Balaam story, found in Numbers 22–24, comes out of the time when Israel was in the midst of its forty-year wilderness pilgrimage between its salvation out of Egypt and its possession of Canaan. Those forty years were a time of testing and growth. The Israelites found out what it meant to trust in God, to be provided for by God, and to hear the word of God and live trusting it. When they were nearing the end of their pilgrimage and ready to enter the new land, they came to a final enemy: Balak, king of the Moabites. Balak was scared. He had heard the reports of this people, divinely preserved through the terrible wilderness, accompanied by a gracious and powerful God. He knew there was nothing he could do to stop them. Desperate for something to stop them, not at all sure that his weapons could do it, he sent for the famous Balaam, a sorcerer. He offered Balaam an enormous fee if he would come and put a curse on Israel.

Balaam knew it was the wrong thing to do and initially refused. But then—his heart not really in his refusal—when his arm was twisted, he agreed. Now the funny part starts. Balaam was riding his donkey, and suddenly the angel of the Lord appeared and blocked the way with a drawn sword in his hand. The donkey swerved out of the road and bolted into the field. Balaam beat his donkey with his staff and got it back onto the road. Then they were in a vineyard along a narrow closed-in path, walled in, and the sword-wielding angel blocked the path again. The donkey tried to get around the angel and crushed Balaam's foot against the wall. Balaam, understandably angry with his donkey, banged on it again with his staff. A few miles down the road, they entered a very narrow passage, and the angel blocked the way a third time. Now there was simply no place to go. The donkey simply lay down.

Now let me paraphrase, the rest of this tale, with only minor liberties. Balaam's patience had run out quite a while back. He lost his temper completely and beat his donkey with his stick, black and blue. The poor donkey had had enough by this time and opened its mouth and said, "What have I done to you that you have beat me three times?" Balaam was so angry and beside himself by this time that he didn't even notice anything unusual in his donkey talking, and he answered back, "Because you are making a donkey out of me, that's why. If I had a sword, I'd kill you on the spot."

The donkey defended itself: "Haven't I been a faithful donkey to you for these many long years? Have I ever made a donkey out of you before? Haven't I always been a good donkey?" And Balaam, calming down a little by now, said, "Well, as a matter of fact, you're right. You have been a good donkey, and you have never made a donkey out of me." And then Balaam saw what the donkey saw—the angel blocking the way with the sharp two-edged sword in his hand—and he heard the angel speak: "Why have you beaten your donkey? It's you I am trying to show that you are not going in the right way. The donkey was bright enough to see me blocking the way. Why weren't you? I thought you were supposed to be a sorcerer, able to figure out the ways of God, and this dumb donkey knows more about God's will than you do."

Balaam offered to go back, but the angel told him that since he was almost where he had set out for to go ahead and see what could be done there. Balak was glad to see him, of course. But Balaam, a bit shaken from his experience on the way, made no promises to him: he told him that he could say only what God gave him to say. But Balak figured that money talked louder than God, and he set things up for a great ritual of cursing.

They climbed a hill from which they could see the people of Israel camped, ready to conquer, below them on the plain. They built seven altars, and on each one they sacrificed a ram and a bull; they burned the offerings, with the great retinue of princes in attendance. The suspense built. I can imagine Balaam concentrating, getting himself into a trance, and then everyone waiting in suspense to hear the great, powerful curses that would dissolve Israel on the plains beneath them. Balaam opened his mouth and began to speak. The people believed that Balak would be triumphant; it was going to work. But he couldn't believe his ears when he heard a great blessing spoken. Balak was beside himself with anger. Balaam said, "I couldn't help it—that is what came out. Let's try again."

So they went to another mountain and did the whole thing over again. They built seven altars, killed a ram and a bull on each one, went through sacrifice rituals, watched Israel down below on the plains, waited as Balaam concentrated and prayed, and got ready for the mystical act of cursing. Balaam opened his mouth and muffed it again.

So they gave it a third try on *another* mountain. Seven more altars, another seven rams and seven bulls. Again, the suspense built. The curse had to work this time. Balaam tried his best to curse, but all he could get out was a blessing: "Blessed be every one who blesses you, and cursed be every one who curses you" (Numbers 24:9). Balak had had it with Balaam, his dumb donkey of a magician: three times he had tried to get him to go down a path of cursing, and three times he had balked and blessed.

But then there's a twist to the story that isn't funny at all. Balaam, having disappointed Balak in the matter of cursing, apparently suggested a way to thwart Israel after all. Instead of cursing Israel, he advised a party with festive food and dancing girls (Numbers 25:1–2; 31:16; Jude 1:11). It worked. The people of Israel, after forty years of austerity in the desert, were seduced by the smell of roasted rams and the smiles of perfumed girls. They had been true to God in matters of life and death but failed to be true in matters of eating and drinking. Opposition didn't work. Cursing didn't work. But clever lies did.

And why bring up this convoluted ancient story? Because the same principle was about to work on one of John's congregations. A hostile society had tried everything to get the Christians to fold, without avail. They were the bravest, most courageous, most steadfast people the world had ever seen. They were persecuted, but they didn't budge an inch. At least one of their number, Antipas, lost his life, like Polycarp years later in the Smyrna church. But the danger was from an unexpected direction: some nice people who were suggesting that it is possible to be just a little too strict with ourselves. After all, what counts is what we believe and our courage in standing up for the right—saying the truth. But in everyday life, we have to get along in the world that we find ourselves in, and we can't be making ourselves obnoxious all the time. If you are going to make people feel ill at ease with you all the time by being a bluenose, is that a very Christian thing to do?

But that is Satan's lie. To separate what we say from the way we live. To make a division between our confession in worship and our conduct at work. Truth is lived truth. Truth is not simply what we say but what we live.

✳ *Truth is not simply what we say but what we live.*

John, pastor to the Pergamene Christians, used Balaam's story to give his parish the truth test: "I have a few things against you: you have some there who hold the teaching of Balaam" (Revelation 2:14). Like the Israelites, they were true to their Lord when the going was tough; they passed the martyr test with flying colors. They didn't give an inch when it was demanded that they curse Christ or die. But when the pressure was off and they entered normal routines of work and play, some suggested they relax just a little. Surely they had proved beyond a shadow of doubt that they were true to Christ. Now it was time to enjoy themselves a little and get along with their neighbors. If they were uptight prudes and puritans, they would not be able to give a very attractive witness to Christ, would they?

Sometimes it is easier to die for the truth in a crisis than to live the truth through a dull week at work. The truth test comes, though, not on the heights to which we rise under pressure but through those ordinary hours when we don't know we are being examined at all. Truth is not just right answers but a right life. Christ is our comprehensive, personal truth to be expressed in gestures, actions, and conversations when no one is watching. It is only the teaching of Balaam that says differently, and we dismissed him with laughter ages ago.

The teaching of Balaam is the kind of teaching that tries to make things easier and clearer than they really are, adds on to the gospel, and elaborates on real truth, God's truth. Gospel truth is always personal, direct, obedient—a way to live in love and courage and adoration. The Greek word for "truth" is interesting: *aletheia**—unhiddenness, evident, manifest, open, present. We find the truth in the everyday, the things evident and manifest that we encounter there in the light that Christ throws on our being, on our lives. The truth test bares our being before Christ's being. We are seen in the concrete, not the abstract—as livers of *this* life, of my life *as it is*. Who we really are is revealed in the light of his life. It is seen in the clarity of his life as it is revealed to us in the Cross and Resurrection. And those great events illuminate the depth and meaning of the things we call "the everyday."

The truth test asks not *What do you think?* but *Who are you?* Not *What is your opinion?* but *What is your decision?* God is not nearly as interested with

---

* Thayer and Smith, "Greek Lexicon Entry for Aletheia," *The NAS New Testament Greek Lexicon,* 1999, www.biblestudytools.com/lexicons/greek/nas/aletheia.html.

what we say *about* him to others as he is with what we say *to* him. When there is truth so that relationship and things are seen as they really are, then is the time to speak of him to others.

The Pergamene Christians lived, their pastor said, where Satan dwells. That provides a clue to their situation. Satan is the Father of Lies. They lived in the place where there was a web of lies—propaganda, deceit, distortion—a city where words were not used to keep people in touch with reality but to manipulate them and confuse them into unreality. Most words are used that way today. Things have not improved, and Christ examines us in the same way.

An urgent promise is given to the Pergamene church, and to us, on the basis of an affirmative response to this sharp two-edged sword of Christ. It is this: "To him who conquers I will give some of the hidden manna, and I will give him a white stone, with a new name written on the stone which no one knows except him who receives it" (verse 17).

The hidden manna is the food that God gives to his people, the nourishment that keeps them going. The stone with the new name written on it is the identification that Christ gives us as his people. He will sustain us, and he will identify us as his own. A most appropriate reward for being victorious in the struggle! The battle is not between good and evil but between truth and error. To fight it well means to throw one's life on the side of truth, to discern between what is right and what is spurious.

God will sustain his truth and confirm its identification. The truth will be energized with the nutriments of the new manna, and it will be validated with the identifying stone.

What we believe makes a difference because what God believes makes a difference. For he is God, and his Word is as sharp and quick as a two-edged sword.

Amen.

THYATIRA

The words of the Son of God, who
has eyes like a flame of fire, and
whose feet are like burnished
bronze. . . . I have this against you:
you tolerate that woman Jezebel.

—Revelation 2:18, 20, NRSV

The Test of Our Holiness

April Fools' Day is an unofficial holiday in the church. Children have a special fondness for it. I know I did. It was marked in my childhood by an outrageous joke played out in my father's butcher shop. Every year, he collaborated with Hank the baker, whose shop was next to ours. They made chocolates that were filled with garlic and set them out on their display counter on a platter. No one was invited to take one. People took them anyway.

Some would react noisily with exclamations. Others, realizing they hadn't been invited to take the candy, pretended nothing was wrong. In these cases, the rule of the store was that we also pretended nothing was wrong. That, to me, left out the best part. I would follow them out of the store, and while they were at the curb getting rid of the gift, I—unable to contain myself—would say, "April Fool!"

In Thyatira, Christians, who were admirable in almost every way, were being made fools of by reaching for attractive-appearing religion that in fact was inwardly foul. We are told, in the Christian way, that we are to be fools for Christ, but that is not quite the same thing as being made a fool *of*.

 Being a fool for Christ means pursuing the reality of God even when the appearance isn't congenial.

Being a fool for Christ means pursuing the reality of God even when the appearance isn't congenial. Being made a fool of means chasing the appearance of religion when inward reality has nothing to do with God.

※

The Christian always lives life out in conscious opposition to the world. The conflict—between what the Christian believes and therefore does and what the world assumes and therefore does—produces in every age a sharp division.

While many believers seem to want to retreat from society, there is no way to be a Christian except in the world. Attempts to escape from our environment have never been successful. Monastic retreats and hermit solitudes have mostly resulted in a distortion of our witness. But though the world is inevitable for the Christian life, it certainly is not helpful to it. Often it is seductive to Christ's purposes. And it *always* contrasts with them. John's letter to the congregation at Thyatira gives us an example of what one group of Christians had to contend with in relation to their society.

Thyatira was a commercial city, strong in trade unionism. In order to work, one had to be a member of one of the guilds. These guilds, which the Christian had no choice but to be a part of, dominated life, but the Christian lived a life that Christ sought to dominate. There was bound to be a conflict of interest.

We look at the Christians in Thyatira and listen to the message to find out what they did in the conflict. Our society is radically different from theirs, but it is of no more help to us. Society has not grown friendlier to the Christian through the ages. With the insight gained by the Thyatira congregation, we will be fortified in our own vision and obedience to our Lord.

Christ is introduced to the Thyatira congregation as "the Son of God, who has eyes like a flame of fire, and whose feet are like burnished bronze" (Revelation 2:18). The eyes like a flame of fire burn as they penetrate. This is no casual survey. The Son of God does not use his eyes as a person who is window-shopping, butterfly hopping from one object to another without giving any real attention to any object, without any seriousness in his gaze. His examination burns into those who meet his gaze. He really sees. The feet like burnished bronze are solid and strong. They will not crumble under opposition. They will not retreat when meeting adversity. He has a base of bronze to reinforce his examination.

The solidity of the bronze feet was achieved by the use of fire—bronze is an alloy made of mixing copper and tin under heat. The combination not only is stronger after the smelting but also has a new melting point. The bronze feet, then, are the necessary foundation for the burning eyes, which will look into opposing and unfriendly situations. Christ is presented to them as the one with penetrating eyes of fire and supported by strong bronze feet tempered with fire and shining in their strength. He sees through all facades, evasions, masks, and fogginess—sees into contradiction, opposition, hostility, and indifference. And his scrutiny is backed up by bronze strength.

Our first response to the prospect of such an examination would be to run for cover. Yet we need not. There is mercy and generosity in the honest, unflinching gaze of our Lord. If his look burns, it is the fire of love, and it burns so that it may warm us.

※ *There is mercy and generosity in the honest, unflinching gaze of our Lord. If his look burns, it is the fire of love, and it burns so that it may warm us.*

Proof of his generosity comes on the first returns of the examination: "I know your works, your love and faith and service and patient endurance, and that your latter works exceed the first" (verse 19). The Thyatiran Christians at least were not resting on past achievements. There was no sitting back and telling stories about how vigorous and exciting it had been in the early days of the church. They had not fallen into the habit (which Christians seem prone to) of lamenting the present evil generation and nostalgically looking back to a better time. They were not like Miniver Cheevy, who

Sighed for what was not,
And dreamed, and rested from his labors;
He dreamed of Thebes and Camelot,
And Priam's neighbors.*

Unlike the congregation at Ephesus, which had lost its first love, the Thyatiran Christians' latter works exceeded their first. They were becoming skilled in and increasingly committed to love, faith, service, and patient endurance.

But the Lord's blazing eyes saw a disturbing element among the virtues. He continued, "I have this against you: you tolerate that woman Jezebel, who calls herself a prophet and is teaching and beguiling my servants to practice fornication and to eat food sacrificed to idols" (verse 20, NRSV).

There was a person in the congregation who was teaching and leading people astray. By being called a Jezebel, she was characterized in a word.† Jezebel was

---

* Scott Donaldson, *Edwin Arlington Robinson: A Poet's Life* (New York: Columbia University, 2007), 246.
† Editor's note: The term *Jezebel* has often been misapplied or used abusively to demean women. Eugene's usage here, in keeping with Saint John's, is focused on the intentional religious deception of the historical Jezebel as a

the most notorious evil woman in Hebrew history. She was the wife of Ahab, one of the weakest kings of Israel. She had imported into Israel an alien cult. Her father, Ethbaal by name, was a priest of Astarte who had succeeded to the throne of Sidon by murdering his predecessor. Astarte was the Phoenician equivalent of the Greek Aphrodite and the Roman Venus. Her beastly system had engineered such a complete divorce of morality from religion that it even encouraged gross sexual immorality under the cloak of piety. According to one etymology, *Jezebel* (like our English *Agnes*) means "pure" or "chaste," but Jezebel contradicted her name by her character and her behavior.[*]

When she married King Ahab, she became active in the diffusion of her revolting doctrines in Israel. She may even have been a priestess of Astarte herself. She persuaded the king to build a temple and altar to Astarte in his capital, Samaria. She supported 850 prophets of her immoral cult and killed off all the prophets of righteous Jehovah on whom she could lay

---

wider spiritual symbol. It should not be read as flippant or intending to direct shame toward women, whom Eugene respected deeply and empowered for ministry throughout his life.

[*] Editor's note: Eugene did not reference this work explicitly, but more context on the name *Jezebel* can be found in Michael J. Wilson, *What the Scriptures Say About Women* (Summerville, SC: Holy Fire, 2007), 97.

her hands. She became well known for what Jehu later called "the many whoredoms and sorceries of . . . Jezebel" (2 Kings 9:22, NRSV). She sought to contaminate Israel, as Balaam had done before her, and Ahab did not possess the moral conviction or stamina to withstand her.

This first Jezebel had been dead nearly a thousand years. She met a horrible end. But her evil spirit had, as it were, become reincarnated in a prophetess of the first century AD. Her religion, too, had little connection with morality. Laying claim to divine inspiration, she was succeeding in beguiling the servants of Christ to indulge in immoral practices. She was encouraging the Christians of Thyatira to attend the ceremonies and feasts of the local trade guilds, which were dedicated to some pagan deity and too often ended in unbridled licentiousness. This new Jezebel and her followers prided themselves on their mature experience of life. They were delving into secret mysteries, of which they boasted a private revelation that had been denied to the rest of the Christians. They were a spiritual aristocracy, a favored elite. The rank and file could not compete with them.

They bragged that they plumbed the deep things. Perhaps they even borrowed this phrase from Saint

Paul, who spoke several times in his epistles of the deep things of God—the deeps of his wisdom and love, which people cannot know but which the Holy Spirit searches out and explores. With Jezebel's diabolical theory that, since matter is evil, the sins of the flesh can be indulged without damage to the spirit, the Christians of Thyatira plunged without restraint into what they called the deep things (of Satan, Christ ironically adds, not of God).

Jezebel's answer to the Christian's conflict with the world was to eliminate the conflict by assimilating the differences. Instead of refusing to participate in what was evil, she taught that the Christian must assimilate all the evil and thereby redeem it. Any examination that we undergo must include an examination of our relation to society. And in particular here, business society. We cannot exclude such a major part of our lives from the probing, searching gaze of Christ. Our tendency is to assimilate, to take on the coloration of those with whom we work—our employers, our companies, our associates. But Christ's command is that we should differentiate.

We live in contrast to them. Clearly we cannot do it by being holier than thou—acting or seeming to be superior. But neither can we do it by acting as if there is no difference, by continually accommodating ourselves to the ethics and the standards of society. For us, I don't think it is a question of unethical business practices. There is, of course, a Christian decision to be made from time to time. But, on the whole, there is a high standard of morality and ethical behavior in contemporary business. Nevertheless, there doesn't seem to be very much Christian self-consciousness in it. There doesn't seem to be the frank affirmation of the Christian to himself, *This is God's work, not the devil's.* There doesn't seem to be the readiness to devote the business day to the glory of God.

Jezebel was the symbolic nickname for the lying teacher who tricked Christians into foolishness. Centuries earlier, the historical Jezebel had introduced a religion into Israel that was glamorous and entertaining. It was all appearance and no substance. It appealed to self-interest, greed, lust. It nearly put Israel under. Jezebel keeps showing up century after century in congregation after congregation. She showed up in Thyatira, and John warned the church. The appeal of the Jezebel lie doesn't fade. In fact, right now we are under a media blitz of Jezebel teaching. It is April Fools' religion and promises two things: to make you feel good and to get you what you want. And what chance does "Deny yourself and take up your cross daily" have against that?

Our every religious appeal and teaching must be put to the test of our holiness. Appearance is no test. Attractiveness is no test. Miracle promises are no test. But sincerity is. And integrity. Are we what we say we are? What is *inside*? Chocolate? Or garlic?

Good questions are rarely easy. But they protect us from being made fools *of*.

※ *Christ, "who searches mind and heart" (Revelation 2:23), sees past religious glamour, a moral front, dazzling entertainment, and God-jargon. He finds that place deep within us where the seed of faith can be planted.*

Ask these simple questions to help evaluate your sincerity: Does this teaching return you to the God revealed in Christ—his words, his acts—or does it excite you with what you'll get, acquire, feel? Does this teaching return you to yourself—who you are, where you are—or does it incite ambition, discontent, a desire to be someone else, somewhere else?

The root of the word *humility* is *humus*—"earth."

Humility is down-to-earthness. Christ, "who searches mind and heart" (Revelation 2:23), sees past religious glamour, a moral front, dazzling entertainment, and God-jargon. He finds that place deep within us where the seed of faith can be planted and cultivated and where foolish-appearing things, like prayer and love and fidelity, strike deep roots in the field of life and become the realities that rule the world.

When our Lord subjects us to an examination, I can hear him using words in the spirit of those to Thyatira:

> I know your works. They are greater than those at first. You work hard—harder every year, far harder than your parents. Your attitude is great—enthusiasm, love, service, patient endurance. You do your work exceedingly well. There is not a lazy person among you. You are energetic and successful, and for that I commend you. But I have this against you: You tolerate Jezebel. You tolerate the assumption that commerce has prior claim on your talents. You unthinkingly take for granted that Christ is not interested in your work. You act as if our Lord never worked as a carpen-

ter in a business world and has no feeling for what you do. You make a religion out of your work, and, however moral and successful it is, it is not the same religion you profess as a Christian.

Jezebel is the symbol for religion separated from God and devoted to success at all costs. Jezebel doesn't persecute the church; she asks only to be tolerated by it. She worships in the church and listens to its sermons. But then she sets herself up as a prophetess and declares her own wisdom to be the standard in the world of work. She takes over. Jezebel must be cast out.

To the Christian who reaffirms his identity and listens to his Lord, there is a double promise. First, "he who conquers and who keeps my works until the end, I will give him power over the nations, and he shall rule them with a rod of iron, as when earthen pots are broken in pieces, even as I myself have received power from my Father" (Revelation 2:26–27). This promise is appropriate for the person who has lived in the midst of a society that has threatened to break him into pieces, to shatter his convictions and remold him on its own principles. He has often felt as if he might be broken by this pressure and opposition. In fact, he maybe has been broken. But Christ tells him, *The future is yours. You shall rule. Your convictions, your living, your uncompromised obedience to me shall prove the stronger will in the end. Not you, but they, shall be broken.*

✳ *Christ promises himself to us as the end*
of the night and the beginning of the
day. Whatever difficulties we have had
in belief and holy living, they are in the
past. His presence will dominate the
days ahead.

This breaking, it must be noted, is not destructive. A society that has become successful in exploiting sin and greed and rebellion cannot be received into the kingdom of God; it must be broken and rebuilt. When this church was built, the first piece of equipment at the site was a bulldozer. It tore out the earth as it was. It realigned the contours of the ground. The earth was not destroyed here, but it was pretty violently rearranged. The bulldozer's apparent destructiveness was necessary preparation for the construction of our church building. Society must finally be broken in this way. If we assimilate society and its principles into ourselves, we will also have to be broken like the ill-formed piece of pottery. If we maintain our convictions in holy living, we can be the agents who reform and rule society.

The second part of the promise is "I will give him the morning star" (verse 28). The morning star is the sign of the dawn. The night has been long and there have been millions of stars shining in the sky, but they have been only pinpoint illuminations of what was basically black night. And then the morning star appears, and we know the dawn is not far off. A flood of brightness comes before the dawning sun.

The morning star is Christ himself. He promises himself to us as the end of the night and the beginning of the day. Whatever difficulties we have had in belief and holy living, they are in the past. His presence will dominate the days ahead. He is here already. He speaks to us in love and judgment.

Obey his voice and receive his love.

Amen.

SARDIS

The words of him who has the seven
spirits of God and the seven stars.
I know your works; you have
the name of being alive, and
you are dead.

—Revelation 3:1

The Test of Our Reality

A number of years ago, a young couple in our church had a child and gave him the shockingly un-Presbyterian name of Wesley. They brought him to worship at an early age, as is our custom here (the importance of children in the act of worship can hardly be overestimated). One Sunday when he was about two years old, Wesley slipped away from his parents while I was in the middle of my sermon, ran behind the pews, and made a dash down the center aisle, positioning himself in cheerful defiance between table and pulpit. His father stood at the back of the church and muttered what I *think* was a prayer.

The scene is a parable. Some people come to church to pray, others to play. Most are here to exercise their faith, but some, usually the more recently baptized, are simply here to have fun. And I wonder in response, *What was Wesley's father praying that Sunday? Why was Wesley having so much fun? Was it a sin for me to enjoy it so much?*

✳ *Playing spills out when we are being ourselves. Praying spills out when we are being more than ourselves.*

The words *playing* and *praying* often sound alike. Their nature is also similar. Playing spills out when we are being ourselves. Praying spills out when we are being more than ourselves. Playing is delight in being in the image God made us. Praying is delight in the God who made us in his image. Wholly alive, we pray and play, seething with vitality *outwardly* and *upwardly*. Virginia Stem Owens wrote,

Either the creator's work is a sign of himself or it's a sham. Where else can one draw the line between sacred and profane except around all the cosmos? For "profane" meant, originally, outside the temple, and all creation was, in the beginning, a temple for God's "very good." Whenever we eat, drink, breathe, see, take anything in by any means, we are commanded to remember the sacrifice. . . .

Still, we take the big black crayon in our hands and draw these little islands where we will let God live in the world. . . . Little concentration camps for Christ.*

The Sardis church was one such "concentration camp." Rather, a death camp. The Sardis church had a reputation for being alive, but it was dead. It was dead because it excluded the everyday world. It gave an impression of vigor—"the name of being alive" (Revelation 3:1)—but the sharp line it drew between everyday life and holy-day life cut the veins and arteries in which the holy blood of our Lord ("for the life . . . is in the blood" (Leviticus 17:11) circulated the cleansing, forgiving, praying life of the Spirit through all play, work, politics, and culture. No children played in the Sardis church, and no adults prayed in the Sardis marketplace. Praying was for church; playing was for outside church.

John called his Sardis congregation to wake up. To be consciously alive to the presence of God at both earth and altar. A few were alive; he described them as

---

* Virginia Stem Owens, *And the Trees Clap Their Hands: Faith, Perception, and the New Physics* (Eugene, OR: Wipf and Stock, 1983), 142.

those "who have not soiled their garments" (Revelation 3:4); that is, they had not polluted or desecrated what God made holy through creation and redemption. Those few experienced the wholeness/holiness of God equally while playing and praying.

I've heard that the words *hail, holy, hello,* and *whole* are all related. Is it possible for us to sing "Hail, Hail, the Gang's All Here" in the same spirit we sing "Holy, Holy, Holy"?

 That is the holiness test: discovering the presence of the holy Christ and the movements of the Holy Spirit in these everyday faces we encounter.

That is the holiness test: discovering the presence of the holy Christ and the movements of the Holy Spirit in these everyday faces we encounter in and out of church, playing and praying together through the whole life that Christ gives us so abundantly.

Christ confronted the church in Sardis as the one who "has the seven spirits of God and the seven stars" (Revelation 3:1). The "seven spirits of God" is the usual symbolic expression in Revelation for what we more usually call the Holy Spirit. This might confuse some of us—we are used to hearing that God is spirit. Of course that is true. But this somewhat poetic affirmation from John that God "has" spirit (seven, to be exact, a symbol of perfection) is one of the most important statements that the church makes. When we say that God has spirit, we mean that he has *life*. The word *spirit* in both Hebrew and Greek (the two biblical languages) means basically "wind" or "breath."* There is something active, energetic, and moving in God. He can be the same, but he is not stuck. He is not static. Don't let the imagery confuse you. It is saying that in God is perfect, moving *life*.

You see how deeply this affects our understanding of God. If God has spirit, then God is not simply an idea or an abstraction. It is popular to say that God is the *idea* of beauty or of love or of truth. Whatever is beautiful or lovely or truthful is God. That is a nice sentiment but poor theology. God is personal and deeply alive.

If God has spirit, he cannot be dealt with only as an element in the past. He is present. Active. Most people

---

* M. G. Easton, s.v. "Spirit," *Illustrated Bible Dictionary*, 3rd ed. (Nashville: Thomas Nelson, 1897), www.biblestudytools.com/dictionary/spirit.

find some satisfaction in thinking that God started all the evolutionary and geological processes that have preceded our present state of existence. God is the creator of the universe. Unfortunately, having put God at the beginning of all things, many of us leave him there. But he will not be left there. He has spirit! He is living and active now with the results of his present being.

If God has spirit, he cannot be dealt with as an object. He must be confronted as a person. A living, personal being demands relationship. I can arrange books, rooms, clothing, and even work, but I must *live* with persons. They resist being put in their place. They refuse to be arranged and manipulated. They must be talked to. There must be an exchange of feelings with them. I have heard the phrase "We must leave a place for God in our lives." This is a nice idea if it would work, but it won't, because God has spirit. He will not be confined to a place. He is a living being with whom we must live. This is part of what it means to say that God has spirit. It means fundamentally that we have the perfection of a living God in our midst.

This living God, this God who has "has the seven spirits of God and the seven stars," examined the Christians in Sardis and said, "I know your works; you have the name of being alive, and you are dead" (verse 1). It is the harshest word we have heard spoken to the churches. From the examining Christ, every one of the other churches heard first a word that was commendatory and encouraging. Only after that did some of them hear the word of judgment. Can it be that in Sardis there was nothing at all to compliment? Was there nothing good at all in the congregation there? They probably were not that bad, but the nature of their failures permitted no other course than to drive to the central situation as quickly as possible.

Sainte-Beuve once commented that in France, people continue to be Catholics long after they cease to be Christians.* That is what happened in Sardis. They were calling themselves church members long after they had ceased being animated by the spirit of Christ.

"You have the name of being alive, and you are dead."

The world is one single whole. It's *holy.*

We divide it into areas marked out for God and areas marked out for ourselves. We call churches sa-

---

cred and playgrounds secular. We have places where we pray and others where we play. But our compartments desecrate the way things are supposed to be; the earth is the Lord's. All of it.

※ *The world is one single whole. It's holy. We divide it into areas marked out for God and areas marked out for our-selves. We call churches sacred and play-grounds secular. We have places where we pray and others where we play. But our compartments desecrate the way things are supposed to be; the earth is the Lord's.*

This whole place is his temple, in which angel hosts are crying out, "Holy, holy, holy" (Revelation 4:8). If we treat any of it—its air, its land, its work, its money—as if it were anything other than holy, we pollute it. We leech the life out of it, and the life we take from it is God's life.

Amen.

PHILADELPHIA

Behold, I have set before you an open
door, which no one is able to shut.

—Revelation 3:8

The Test of Our Witness

Spike was the big kid who lived in the corner house. He knew everything about everything. I admired him extravagantly and always felt honored when he paid attention to me. He was already a veteran in exploring the wide world, having nearly completed the first grade. I was four years old. One day he announced that we were going to find some Indians who had set up their tepee in the woods.* He warned that it was dangerous. Scalpings, he said, were not unheard of. Was I up to it? I didn't hesitate. The parental command

---

* Editor's note: To balance this dated cultural depiction, it is important to note the deep respect with which Eugene spoke of Native Americans throughout his private and public life. I've elected to retain this boyhood story, which reflects common twentieth-century stereotypes, in keeping with Eugene's intention in preaching it—to highlight the human desire for more.

not to leave the street didn't stand a chance against the lure of the wild. Keeping rules was for wimps. I, inspired by Spike's bravado, was bursting with courage.

A few hours later when we were caught (not by Indians but by our parents), we found that it was easier to be brave with imagined Indians than with actual parents.

What is there in us that stretches beyond the security of home and impels us to danger? The desire for more is very strong in us.

Unfortunately, the desire can be manipulated by cowards and seducers who themselves risk nothing. And sadly, our expansive spirits can be curbed by a lazy hankering after security. Christ promises security: "You will find rest for your souls" (Matthew 11:29). He also calls us beyond security to hazard: "I send you out as sheep in the midst of wolves" (10:16). He gives us the best he has. He also gets the best out of us. He saves us. He also sends us. He cares for us, but he also challenges us. He appeals to the same thing in us that my erstwhile friend Spike appealed to, but he does it differently. Christ accompanies us, courageous to the end.

Jesus could have continued his Galilean ministry indefinitely, healing and helping and teaching to applause. But there was more. There was Jerusalem. One day he left the security of Galilee success and entered the danger of Jerusalem testing. He was met with enthusiasm. I wonder how many of those palm-waving children had ventured from the security of their courtyards, sensing Jesus's brave courage and wanting to be in on it.

Sixty years later, through John, Jesus wrote to the church at Philadelphia, "I have set before you an open door" (Revelation 3:8). You thought you were snug in the arms of Jesus, secure from now to eternity? Surprise. There is more—a trial and a cross.

 ✳ *Will you go through the open door? Or*
 will you huddle in the comfort of religion?

There are sacrifices to be made, enemies to love, friends to serve, the poor to help, prisoners to visit, ignorance to confront, cruelty to oppose, hypocrisy to unmask. An open door to the people who need us, to the world where others are waiting for a credible witness and a committed friend. Will you go through the open door? Or will you huddle in the comfort of religion? That is the bravery test, the test of our witness. John detected a tendency in his Philadelphia congregation toward taking it easy. They had been through persecution and martyrdom and were now settling down to enjoy the comfort of their shepherd Lord. But it wasn't retirement time yet.

A fear of the unknown must not set boundaries for our lives. An overweening desire for comfort must not inhibit our appetites for danger. The life of Christ is not complete in us when we have received it but only when we risk it against lies and indifference and evil. The same open door that Christ went through on Palm Sunday is still open.

Missions is not quite the right word. It has been spoiled by Michener and Maugham.* All the missionaries I have known have been exciting, courageous persons, while all the missionaries I read about in novels are dogmatic, narrow, opinionated rascals. So *missions* as a word has got to go.

But how about *missiles*? This word comes from the same Latin root referring to something thrown or sent.†

---

* Editor's note: Eugene is likely referencing the 1959 novel *Hawaii* by James A. Michener and the 1921 short story "Rain" by W. Somerset Maugham. Both feature the relationships, sometimes tragic, of out-of-touch missionaries with the people they have been sent to convert.

† *Merriam-Webster,* s.v. "missile," www.merriam-webster.com/dictionary /missile.

For me it has all the original aura of excitement, skill, and the latest in contemporary thinking. It is possible to think of ourselves (imaginatively) as missiles—projectile persons—capable of being sent to a destination at the direction of Christ.

Philadelphia (not the city in Pennsylvania but the one in Turkey) was set on the ancient frontier as a missile city. It was established at the edge of a barbarian wilderness to serve as a launching point for Greek culture to the hinterland. Those who originally settled in Philadelphia were there to be sent into the inland country with the purpose of spreading Greek culture. It was a city with an open door.

The church in Philadelphia found itself also on a frontier. The message to their church capitalizes on the history of their city and applies the same purpose to the broader Christian church. The Christian does not find himself, after being accepted by God, in a comfortable luxury hotel, smoking big cigars and reading the newspapers. He is a missile—a man destined to be sent through the open door into the society of the world to share the meaning of love and grace.

We remember Palm Sunday when we think of "sentness." That day, Jesus went through an open door into Jerusalem. Jesus for three years had engaged in a ministry that could be done outside Jerusalem. He healed sick people in the villages, he comforted people in the homes of their bereavement, and he taught crowds on pastoral hillsides. All these activities that we often think of as the characteristic acts of Jesus could be carried on outside Jerusalem. He helped, he healed, he taught, and he represented God to us. But there was one major act left to do. And it could take place only in Jerusalem.

Jesus needed to proclaim his rule to the people. This act needed Jerusalem for its location because Jerusalem was the center of the area, in some ways the center of the world. What good would it do to rule from a provincial Galilee or from some washed-out village on the Jordan? If he was to represent the rule of God over all, he would have to show that symbolically by ruling from Jerusalem.

✳ *Christ lived for the open door—to enter Jerusalem and our lives, to assert the rule of God over all creation.*

And so Christ entered Jerusalem, riding on a colt. He was the first one since Solomon to enter Jerusalem like that, and the parallelism wasn't lost on the people. They saw the point of his entrance and proclaimed with great joy his rule over them: "Hosanna!" When Christ entered, he entered to rule as the king. Not just to teach, not just to heal, not just to help, not even to remind the people of the nature of God—but to rule.

Christ invaded this world to finally rule over us. He was the missile of God with purpose and destination. We hear a lot about UFOs and aliens these days. Behind the fascination with them and all the speculation, there reappears from time to time an eerie feeling that perhaps *someone,* some other creature capable of ruling over us, is about to impose a new authority over us, about to take over. And we are fearful of that. Maybe some of the same avoidance is in our thinking about Christ. He came to rule. Christ lived for the open door—to enter Jerusalem and our lives, to assert the rule of God over all creation.

As I see it, there are three possible reactions when the rule of Christ enters our sphere: joy, weeping, and anger. They are not necessarily mutually exclusive.

First, *joy*. Those ruled by God are in tune with him and living the fullness of their lives. Christ himself is an example of remarkable joy and celebration at many moments in his ministry. His kingdom rule brings joy.

But there is also *weeping when his rule encounters an obstacle in the human heart.* Jesus wept when he looked over Jerusalem and recalled the massive indifference of the city to the claims of God upon it. He knew that their indifference to his rule and the prophets who preceded him would mean great suffering for them. There was no alternative but to lament and mourn. We should look to him for an example.

And finally there is occasionally *anger in the face of injustice or the cheapening of what is sacred for profit.* Remember that the rule of God meant the cleansing of the temple. Many of the things that people had been doing up to that point could be done no longer, so Jesus threw them out. He was angry, and rightfully so.

So for us, the rule of Christ is not all joy. There is weeping and anger too. But for people under Christ's rule, even in this troubled world, joy is dominant.

The promise to the church in Philadelphia that goes through this open door is this: "He who conquers, I will make him a pillar in the temple of my God; never shall he go out of it" (Revelation 3:12). Philadelphia was an earthquake city. The population repeatedly had to run out of the city when the earthquake tremors began. Sometimes they seemed to be living in a perpetual escape from destruction. To them came this promise (I paraphrase): "You who go through this open door become the missile of Christ; you will finally be established in a certain place where you will have to go out no longer. You will be a pillar."

※ *With the command of the open door be-fore us, with the example of Christ, who entered into our existence through the open door of Jerusalem, we must pray from deeply felt conviction, "Rule over us, Christ our king."*

Our church has long emphasized the primacy of the rule of God over all people in all areas of their lives—economic, social, political, religious. Our church picked up the emphasis in our name, "Christ Our King." With the command of the open door before us, with the example of Christ, who entered into our existence through the open door of Jerusalem, we must pray from deeply felt conviction, "Rule over us, Christ our king."

Amen.

LAODICEA

I know your works: you are neither
cold nor hot. Would that you were
cold or hot! So, because you are
lukewarm, and neither cold nor hot,
I will spew you out of my mouth.

—Revelation 3:15–16

The Test of Our Commitment

John the apostle was the first person to believe in the resurrection of Jesus. Mary and Peter were the first to see the evidence, but it was John who made the leap of faith from the empty tomb to the risen Christ. John's Easter morning belief radiated outward and gathered the despair, guilt, futility, and skepticism of person after person into living praise of this alive and present Savior.

Sixty years later, John the pastor was still presenting this same resurrection event with undiminished fervor to steady, encourage, and motivate his seven congregations of Christians through difficult times. The first Easter morning was an explosion of energy. Did it have detonative power sixty years later? Does it have it still, two thousand years later? It did and it does.

Because it must. For even though the Resurrection doesn't grow dim, we do. We lose our fervor. Especially when we get what we call a well-off life, we lose touch with the elemental, personal, and essential glories of God and our own terrifying needs. We become like the Laodiceans: neither cold nor hot but a comfortable and civilized lukewarm.

The Resurrection? Oh yeah, an important doctrine but unfortunately rather clouded by controversy. Easter? Certainly a significant holiday, and the pagan parallels are interesting too!

Laodicea, the location of the seventh of John's churches, was the only congregation of the seven where it was not dangerous to be a Christian. Unlike with the others, there is no mention in this message of suffering or martyrdom. Lucky Laodiceans! Those Christians enjoyed what Americans take for granted: freedom to worship, safety from persecution.

There is another similarity to American conditions—it was a consumer society. Archaeologists have poked around in Laodicea, and historians have sifted through old documents and found that it was a banking center, a fashion center, and a medical center. The combination of money, fashion, and medicine made Laodicea a good place to live.

As the years went by, a terrible thing happened to the Christians of Laodicea. They became more influenced by their affluent culture than by the Cross. They became consumers. They began to treat Christ as a consumer item. They invested in religion the way they invested in the financial market. They shopped for religion the way they shopped for clothes. They used religion the way they used medicine. They treated Christ with the cool calculation of consumers.

✳ *As the years went by, a terrible thing happened to the Christians of Laodicea. They became more influenced by their affluent culture than by the Cross. They became consumers.*

Do we? John interrupts our tepid consumer mentality with an urgent word from the risen Christ: "Behold, I stand at the door and knock; if any one hears my voice and opens the door, I will come in to him and eat with him, and he with me" (Revelation 3:20).

Here is the passion test. We cannot be lukewarm spectators before such a Christ. We can be only passionate participants or ice-cold deniers. We can keep him at arm's length for only so long—his persistent knocking rouses us to respond. The moment we do, he is in and we are head over heels in love, invaded by our Lord, somersaulted into a life of praise by the power of the Resurrection.

⁕ *We cannot be lukewarm spectators before such a Christ. We can be only passionate participants or ice-cold deniers.*

As we've moved quietly through these letters from John to his beloved congregations, we have voluntarily submitted to an examination by Christ. We've considered the deep insights and questions posed by these letters to first-century churches. As we know, Christ "stood" in the midst of each congregation and examined its works, then commended or condemned the Christians in those seven cities, depending on what the examination revealed.

But what of us? My prayer and hope are that we have been caught by the intense seriousness of our Lord's words and have been impressed by their relevance to us. Christ is examining *us* in specific ways, and we have been given warm words of commendation, sharp reproofs, and urgent promises. It is nearly two thousand years after these original words were written. But the testing is still needed. Particularly, the testing of our *commitment*.

With this in mind, we now read the last letter, the letter to the Laodiceans.

The examining Christ is described as "the Amen, the faithful and true witness, the beginning of God's creation" (verse 14). "Amen" means the affirmation, the yes of God, the certainty and guarantee of God. "Faithful and true witness" certifies his reliability as the Word of God. "Beginning of God's creation," or, as some translators prefer, "source of everything there is," puts him as that one outside which nothing can exist—the origin of existence.

These three descriptions together give us a Christ who includes all reality, behind whose back nothing is done, who doesn't leave out a thing. He is described this way because the people he was to examine thought they had developed a way of life that was pretty satisfactory apart from God. For them, God existed, but on the periphery. They were not deniers of religion; they simply kept religion in its place.

They were the kind of people who would say, *But there is so much to do and know and possess. I cannot confine myself by religion. It is such a narrowing dogma. It is too stifling for words. Not that I don't see the use of it, you know. I want my children to be in Sunday school, and I attend church myself pretty regularly—but I'm a modern, cultivated person. I have a lot of other interests. I certainly don't want to be fanatic about it.* These are the people Christ confronted, and he confronted them in massive dimensions.

However affirmative their lives were, he is more. He is the Amen. However life loving they appeared to be, he is more so. He is the faithful and true witness. However inclusive their lives attempted to be, he is even more inclusive. He is the source of all creation. Nothing escapes him. And this all-inclusive, cosmopolitan Christ examined the Laodicean sophisticates—the people German theologian Schleiermacher called religion's "cultured despisers."*

His examination of their lives was harsh: "I know your works: you are neither cold nor hot. Would that you were cold or hot! So, because you are lukewarm, and neither cold nor hot, I will spew you out of my mouth" (verses 15–16). This is the sternest word that

---

* Friedrich Schleiermacher, *On Religion: Speeches to Its Cultured Despisers,* ed. Richard Crouter, 2nd ed. (Cambridge: Cambridge University, 1996).

came to any of the seven churches. It was a severe word provoked not by (note this well) any flagrant sin, horrible heresy, or cowardly defection. It was provoked by their insipidity. As John Stott wrote, "Jesus Christ would prefer us to boil or freeze, rather than simmer down into a tasteless tepidity."*

The accusatory examination comes perilously close to home. Laodicean lukewarmness seems to be characteristic of the church in our times. Sometimes it seems to me that if you are interested in being hotly fanatic about Jesus Christ, you join one church. If you are icily frigid to him, you join another. But if you are merely lukewarm, you join the Presbyterians. Yet I am sure that is an unfair view, for conversation with other pastors of other churches reveals the same opinion, only in relation to their own denominations. Lukewarmness is not just a Presbyterian trait; it is a human trait.

What is behind this lukewarmness? In one word, *prosperity.*

The Laodiceans were citizens of an affluent society,

---

* John Stott, *What Christ Thinks of the Church: Preaching from Revelation 1 to 3* (Carlisle, UK: Langham Preaching Resources, 2019), 89.

quite as much as we are. Their social and economic situation closely parallels our own, and the identical spiritual condition is the product.

Laodicea was a notably wealthy city, easily the wealthiest of the seven in eastern Asia Minor. Its wealth was based on three things. First, it was a banking center. The banking arrangements for that part of the world were made there, and coins were minted there. It was a combination of Wall Street and Fort Knox.

※ *What is behind this lukewarmness? In one word,* prosperity. *Lukewarmness is the special fault of the successful.*

Second, it was also a garment center. The hills around Laodicea were famous for a certain breed of black-wooled sheep. From this wool, garments and carpeting were manufactured in Laodicea. Fashions were created there, in this mixture of a Paris salon and New York's Fifth Avenue.

Third, it was a medical center. There was a medical school there, which had a worldwide reputation for two locally produced medicines. One was an ointment of nard, which was used to cure sore ears. But above all, it was famous for a certain eye powder. It was exported in tablet form, and the tablets were ground down and applied to the eyes as a cure for ophthalmia. It was a Johns Hopkins Hospital and Mayo Clinic to the ancient world.

Money, fashion, medicine—these three successes brought the Laodiceans affluence and prosperity. They were so completely successful in these material blessings that they quite forgot about any other aspects of the world or existence. They were anesthetized by their affluence, and they lost all sense of God.

There was no need in a city like Laodicea for extreme exertion, for enthusiasm, for zeal. All that was behind them, as they were living comfortably on the plateau of success. They were neither cold nor hot. They were lukewarm.

Lukewarmness is the special fault of the successful. Those who have achieved or inherited are particularly prone to it. It is a basic threat to our church and our Christian faith in these times.

The risen Christ said to the Laodicean church,

> You say, I am rich, I have prospered, and I need nothing; not knowing that you are wretched, piti-

able, poor, blind, and naked. Therefore I counsel you to buy from me gold refined by fire, that you may be rich, and white garments to clothe you and to keep the shame of your nakedness from being seen, and salve to anoint your eyes, that you may see. (Revelation 3:17–18)

How appropriately our Lord counseled them! They thought they were rich with their banks and hoards of money, when in reality they were poor and wretched. So, "get some gold from Christ." They thought they were fashionably clothed with their classy black wool clothes, yet inwardly they were shamefully naked. So, "get some white garments from Christ." They thought they had the best eyesight in the world and the sure cure for any ailments of vision. But they were so blind that they could not see even God. So, "come to Christ for some eye salve so that your vision may be healed."

The plain fact is that a person cannot live without God. But to live with God means to be God dominated. Christ did not condemn the Laodiceans' affluence; he did not decry their prosperity. We sometimes hear the Christian life described in such a way that in order to be a saint, one must be poor, and conversely, to be rich practically eliminates someone from any serious consideration as a faithful disciple of Christ. But Christ did not imply that. He had nothing derogatory to say about their money or their fine clothes or their medicines.

> *The plain fact is that a person cannot*
> *live without God. But to live with God*
> *means to be God dominated.*

But he mercilessly stripped from them the illusion that any of these things have any eternal value. And he harshly rebuked them for allowing such things to divert their attention from God in their lives and lull them into a somnambulant ease separated from any obediently vigorous response to Christ. "Those whom I love, I reprove and chasten; so be zealous and repent" (verse 19).

One of the final verses of the message to the Laodiceans gives one of the most beautiful invitations in Scripture: "Behold, I stand at the door and knock; if any one hears my voice and opens the door, I will come in to him and eat with him, and he with me" (Revelation 3:20).

With all the rebuke and censure and violent language, there is no force at the end. Our Lord stands to be invited in. He will not barge into anyone's life. He knocks courteously. As Saint Francis of Assisi is said to have stated, "God is always courteous and will not invade the privacy of any human soul."*

George MacDonald put it this way:

Nor will God force any door to enter in. He may send a tempest about the house; the wind of his admonishment may burst doors and windows, yea, shake the house to its foundations; but not then, not so, will he enter. The door must be opened by the willing hand, ere the foot of Love will cross the threshold. He watches to see the door move from within. Every tempest is but an assault in the siege of love. The terror of God is but the other side of his love; it is love outside the house, that would be inside—love that knows the house is no house, only a place, until it enter—no home, but a tent, until the Eternal dwell there.†

---

* Editor's note: Though this quote is frequently referenced in sermons and attributed to Saint Francis, the original source is notoriously elusive. Among other places, it is referenced in *The Interpreter's Bible,* ed. George Arthur Buttrick, vol. 8, *Luke and John* (New York: Abingdon, 1952), 323. Buttrick was one of Eugene's key pastoral influences.

† George MacDonald, *Unspoken Sermons* (New York: Cosimo Classics, 2007), 156–57.

There are two things we as a church do, which are illuminated by the scripture we have been reading. One is the service of confirmation. In that service, young people from our congregation make their profession of faith in Jesus Christ and promise to be faithful disciples, to obey his Word, and to show his love. As they make this act of commitment to wholehearted response to Christ, they remind us all of the call to discipleship that our Lord speaks personally to each of us.

Second is the sacrament of the Lord's Supper. As we receive the sacrament, we are receiving Christ. We are responding to his knocking at the door of our lives. We are saying yes to his request to come "into" us, to enter our interior lives and sup with us. As we take in the bread and wine, we are taking the whole Christ into our lives.

Confirmation runs into communion. Discipleship becomes fellowship.

The call to commitment is followed by the invitation to the Lord's Supper. We remember with special poignancy the Last Supper of our Lord. On that night, commitment and communion were inextricably joined.

Yes, there was betrayal at the table as Judas slipped out, unwilling to go all the way in commitment. But there was also a great exchange of *strength* at the table.

All the disciples were weak and faithless. But their weak commitments were confirmed at the table—and as they received Christ and followed him, they grew in stature. They went from strength to strength. Our Lord knocked at their lives, they opened, and he entered.

Let us do the same.

Amen.

THIS HALLELUJAH BANQUET

The angel said to me, "Write this:
Blessed are those who are invited to
the marriage supper of the Lamb."
And he said to me, "These are
true words of God."

—Revelation 19:9

The Supper of the Lamb:
A Benediction

When I was a boy, I found a pocketknife in the woods. It was rusted and dirty. With some difficulty I got the blade open, only to find it was blunt. A thoroughly useless knife. I brought it home and showed it to my grandfather. He started to work on it, soaking it in oil. He rubbed it on a stone; he ground it and polished it. And I watched with delight.

When he was done, the rusty, blunt, dirty knife was shining, sharp, and useful.

Recently I found two words and a blessing. I found them tucked away in Revelation 19. As words go, they have lost their sharpness, their shine. They are blunt, hidden under an accumulation of debris in the last book of the Bible. I am going to try applying some of my grandfather's restoration skills on these words. They are great words. Used with their original sharpness and accuracy, they will make your participation in the life of Christ deeper and better.

The first word is *hallelujah*. Do you remember how many times that word occurs in the New Testament? That's right—four times. And *only* in this passage from Revelation. That is surprising, isn't it? The word is one of the most used religious words in our vocabulary. It has passed from the church into the secular world. There are Broadway plays that use the word, and pop songs. Sometimes it is heard without any church or religious associations, as a simple expression of delight. And all of that is based on these few verses at the back of the Bible (besides its use in the Psalms).

Hallelujah is a Hebrew word meaning, literally, "praise God."* But it has crossed the language barriers and ethnic boundaries and kept its own sound through it all: *hallelujah*. The word has lilt and exuberance to it. Its meaning is expressed in its sounds: *hallelujah*. There

---

* M. G. Easton, s.v. "Hallelujah," *Illustrated Bible Dictionary*, 3rd ed. (Nashville: Thomas Nelson, 1897), www.biblestudytools.com/dictionary/hallelujah.

are happiness and delight in it. Praise is supported by the liquid, undulating sounds of the syllables.

But it is not just a pleasant sound that is preserved in this great word. There is also a rooted experience. God is praised in the word. When we say *hallelujah*, we are participating in the basic experience of joy and gratitude, centering our lives in an open, glad response to God.

We were not created for curse and gloom. We were not put together to live in despair and melancholy. We do not have the natural equipment for blasphemy and bitterness. Every language has its own special vocabulary for cursing, but the vocabulary for praise transcends them all. The curse is provincial. Praise is universal. Swearing is a small-town vice. Praising is a worldwide virtue. Rejection of life is temporary and fleeting and sick. Gratitude for it is deep and pervasive and healthy.

If you want to swear, you have to learn a new word in every language: Hebrew, Greek, Sanskrit, Egyptian, French, Spanish, German, Icelandic, and Russian. If you want to say, "Praise God," one word will do all over the world: *hallelujah*.

Small evidence, perhaps, but significant that it is not the word but the experience that is universal and basic. It is also an adequate explanation for why the four occurrences of *hallelujah* in the Bible infected all the languages of the world with the contagious sound of praising God.

It would be easy to discount the significance of the word if it were said in a burst of good feeling on a summer day by a person well fed and securely stationed. It would express her feelings accurately, but it would not say anything about life as a whole. What would she be able to say when she was ill or oppressed or suffering or exhausted? Would *hallelujah* still be in her vocabulary then? To know the significance of a word, you have to know who says it and the circumstances in which she says it.

Hallelujah was injected into the vocabulary of the peoples of the world by persons who were threatened daily with torture and death. The songs of Revelation were sung by the Christians who lived under the sadism of the Roman police state. The church that sang the hallelujah songs in Revelation was almost exclusively made up of the poor and the exploited, the imprisoned and the martyred.

That means there must be something basically authentic about that which the word expresses. Saying *hallelujah* does not depend, in other words, on a good digestion or a guaranteed annual income. It does not depend on health or security. The word is there because God is here and life is shaped by God for eternal goodness. Grace and love are the centers of existence. *Hallelujah* expresses gratitude toward that reality. You don't have to wait until you feel good to say *hallelujah*. And you don't have to wait until you are good to say it. You can say it now and begin to shape your language and your life around the truth of God in your personal history. Language, if it is going to be useful, has to reflect the reality of life. God is the reality of life. *Hallelujah* is a good word to describe our knowledge and response to that reality.

＊ *You don't have to wait until you feel good to say* hallelujah. *And you don't have to wait until you are good to say it. You can say it now and begin to shape your language and your life around the truth of God.*

The second word is *amen*. It is also an untranslated Hebrew word. And it means "yes."[*] Like *hallelujah*, it

---

[*] "Why Do We Say 'Amen'? What Does It Mean?," Christianity.com, August 21, 2019, www.christianity.com/wiki/christian-life/why-do-we-say -amen-what-does-it-mean.html.

has infiltrated the vocabularies of the peoples of the world. None of you know what the word for "no" is in Hebrew, but you know what "yes" is. You have been saying it all your life, in church and out of it. *Amen—yes*—is God's favorite word.

Paul said this with wonderful directness when he was writing to the Corinthians:

The Son of God, Jesus Christ, whom we pro-claimed among you, Silvanus and Timothy and I, was not "Yes" and "No"; but in him it is always "Yes." For in him every one of God's promises is a "Yes." For this reason it is through him that we say the "Amen," to the glory of God. (2 Corinthians 1:19–20, NRSV)

The gospel, Paul was saying, is not half-negative and half-positive. It is yes. God does not deny your life; he affirms it. The work of Christ is not to qualify and inhibit and diminish your life; it is to accept and release and augment it. The word to you is *yes—amen*.

That being the case, how did we develop so many negative words and feelings? I really don't know. It would take a team of psychiatrists and sociologists to find out. But right now, I'm not terribly interested in the why. What is blazingly clear is that whenever there is repression or negativism or denial, it is not the gospel. It is not the church of Jesus Christ. It is not God's word to us. It is some kind of faithless, small-minded, sinful intrusion into the sacred courts of God's yes.

✳ *What is blazingly clear is that whenever there is repression or negativism or denial, it is not the gospel. It is not the church of Jesus Christ. It is not God's word to us. It is some kind of faithless, small-minded, sinful intrusion into the sacred courts of God's yes.*

No is a word that cannot be fit into the lyrics of worship while the yes is everywhere. I am not, of course, saying (and neither does Scripture) that everything that is, is good, or that anything goes, or that everyone should be encouraged to do whatever he wants to do. I am not saying there is no need for regulation or discipline or judgment. What I am saying is that the basic, overwhelming, eternally fixed word of God to you is yes. Yes, I love you. Yes, I accept you. Yes, I want you. And that our best word back to God is yes. *Amen.*

We have recently had some confusion at our dinner

table with the word *amen*. There has been some difference of opinion on whether to say "ah-men" or "ay-men." My authority in the matter does not seem to have settled the question (a prophet without honor in his own country, you know), and so the differences have persisted. Our youngest, who normally says the table prayers, gets mixed up: ah-men, ay-men. The other day he said, "What does *amen* mean, anyway?" My wife explained that it is the Hebrew word that simply means "Yes, I affirm that too; I agree with that." So when he prays and all the rest of us conclude by saying *amen*, we are saying, "Yes, that prayer you prayed is my prayer too. I am in favor of that." So he said, "Well, why don't we just say yes, then?" The logic is unassailable, so why not? So now we do. Now, in addition to the Hebrew *amen*, we conclude prayers around our table with the English *yes*.

And now the blessing: "The angel said to me, 'Write this: Blessed are those who are invited to the marriage supper of the Lamb.' And he said to me, 'These are true words of God'" (Revelation 19:9). This blessing follows the hymns that feature *hallelujah* and *amen*. The kind of life that expresses gratitude to God and responds with a yes to God is finally gathered around

God's table. Being invited to that table is the best thing that can happen to you. It is God's blessing.

When you are invited to a supper table, you are invited to receive the gift of your host's food and friendship. Nobody pays for a dinner to which she is invited. And ordinarily there is something more than just eating that goes on at the table: there is conversation, the sharing of lives, the establishment of a community.

A marriage supper brings the additional mark of festivity and celebration. The dinner is not only an occasion for gaining strength from food, for sharing a meal and emotional lives in conversation; it is more importantly a celebration for a union, a marriage that has been established by love and commitment. At the marriage supper, love is celebrated in all its joy, and faithfulness is celebrated in all its firmness. Joy and affirmation are celebrated—*hallelujah* and *amen* are united in a festival.

The marriage supper of the Lamb is all this, with the additional factor that it is God himself who is the meal. The lamb—an image for the One who was killed in order to provide for the redemption of all people, the helpless victim who became the victorious conqueror—this lamb, this Christ, this God is the meal. The marriage supper of the Lamb is what we anticipate as we join in worldwide communion. The *hallelujah* and the *amen* are combined in a celebration meal. Our deepest capacity for praise and our deepest impulse for affirmation are focused at this table, where God's goodness and God's yes are expressed in the sacrament. Two words and a blessing. An invitation to eat at God's table. Polish up your *hallelujah*.

Come to this hallelujah banquet of our Lord and be blessed.

This is the end where we make our beginning.

The end from which we start.

Amen.

FINAL EXAMS

Examine your motives, test your
heart, come to this meal in holy awe.

—1 Corinthians 11:28, MSG

About the Final Exams

Eugene H. Peterson hated any recipe for spiritual life, believing it was in our specific time, place, and context that the life of Christ would be slowly and graciously worked into maturity.

With that in mind, this guide is for prayerful introspection rather than being a quick fix for easy growth. Our prayer is that it helps you apply the insights of this book to where you are today, engaging mind and spirit with hopeful honesty.

A Guide for Lent or
Other Times of Renewal

In spring the days lengthen. The air warms. We abandon the survival tactics of winter and look around to see what is going on. We stretch ourselves and feel the juices of love, of faith, of hope rise in our lives.

Christians do not only survive; we grow. But what are the signs of growth? What happens in us as we work and worship, play and talk, shop and sleep, laugh and cry? We get up in the morning and go to bed each night, day after day, week after week. Spring comes around again. A thaw begins in the winter of our sins. We are conscious of being moved by the rhythm of leaf bud and birdsong.

We freshly confess Christ as our savior. We affirm our faith in God. We take a look at ourselves. We ask hard questions: Is our declaration of faith perfunctory or life shaping? Are our prayers pious asides to the eternal, or are they deep inner currents of conversation with God that move us out of our ego orbit into the mainstream of growth and redemption?

Christians have a long tradition of examining ourselves in these matters. Lent is the season for it—spring renewal brought inward. We measure ourselves against the health and holiness of Jesus Christ to find out how far we have come, how far we have to go. How much have we learned? How much have we grown? Are we any closer to maturity now than this time last year? Have we advanced in our commitment? Have we developed in our faith? Or are we stuck in some comfortable self-deception, some cozy self-indulgence?

The purpose of inner examination is not to gloomily document our depravity but to provide clear-sighted self-knowledge for affirmation, for correction, and for motivation. What's right with us? What's wrong with us? What does God have in mind for us?

We will all, finally, stand before the judgment seat of Christ. Our regular final exams (whether in Lent or anytime we need them) are preparation for that time.

Examining Our Love

"Love is not what we do after we get the other things done, if we have any energy left over. Love is what we do, period. It is not how we work; it is our work. Other things can support it, they can grow out of it, and they can lead up to it. But if we don't love, we aren't doing what we were created and saved to do" (page 36).

"Have you strayed from your first love of Christ and those early bursts of love for your neighbors?" (pages 43–44). What might it look like to return to it?

Examining Our Suffering

"I live in a culture and a society where hardly anyone knows the meaning of the word *sacrifice*, where suffering is something to be avoided at all costs and complained of when it can't be avoided, and where it is unthinkable that there is anything more important than preserving and extending my life" (page 54).

"Are you willing to die for your faith? And are you willing to give up anything along the way in order to pursue it—those little deaths that sometimes seem as difficult as the final one, dying to impulses of ambition, of lust, of pride, of security, of comfort?" (pages 55–56).

Examining Our Truth

"Sometimes it is easier to die for the truth in a crisis than to live the truth through a dull week at work. The truth test comes, though, not on the heights to which we rise under pressure but through those ordinary hours when we don't know we are being examined at all" (page 83).

"The truth test asks not *What do you think?* but *Who are you?* Not *What is your opinion?* but *What is your decision?*" (page 84). How well is your heart aligning with your mind?

Examining Our Holiness

"Being a fool for Christ means pursuing the reality of God even when the appearance isn't congenial. Being made a fool of means chasing the appearance of religion when inward reality has nothing to do with God" (page 90).

"Does this teaching return you to the God revealed in Christ—his words, his acts—or does it excite you with what you'll get, acquire, feel? Does this teaching return you to yourself—who you are, where you are—or does it incite ambition, discontent, a desire to be someone else, somewhere else?" (page 99).

Examining Our Reality

"This whole place is his temple, in which angel hosts are crying out, 'Holy, holy, holy' (Revelation 4:8). If we treat any of it—its air, its land, its work, its money—as if it were anything other than holy, we pollute it. We leech the life out of it, and the life we take from it is God's life" (page 114).

"The words *hail, holy, hello,* and *whole* are all related. Is it possible for us to sing 'Hail, Hail, the Gang's All Here' in the same spirit we sing 'Holy, Holy, Holy'?" (page 110). How well are you embracing the sacred nature of everyday life? In what deeper ways is Christ inviting you to encounter the world with earthy wonder and holy love?

Examining Our Witness

"A fear of the unknown must not set boundaries for our lives. An overweening desire for comfort must not inhibit our appetites for danger. The life of Christ is not complete in us when we have received it but only when we risk it against lies and indifference and evil" (page 120).

Christ puts before us "an open door to the people who need us, to the world where others are waiting for a credible witness and a committed friend. Will you go through the open door? Or will you huddle in the comfort of religion?" (page 119).

Examining Our Commitment

"We cannot be lukewarm spectators before such a Christ. We can be only passionate participants or ice-cold deniers. We can keep him at arm's length for only so long—his persistent knocking rouses us to respond" (pages 131–132).

Prayerfully consider your heart. Where has your faith grown passive or complacent? Without shame or fear, consider what deeper invitation to passionate life that Christ might be extending to you at this time in your life.

ABOUT THE AUTHOR

EUGENE H. PETERSON, translator of *The Message: The Bible in Contemporary Language,* is the beloved author of more than thirty books, including *A Long Obedience in the Same Direction, Run with the Horses, As Kingfishers Catch Fire,* and *A Month of Sundays.* He earned his master's degree in Semitic languages from Johns Hopkins University and also held several honorary doctorates. Peterson was the founding pastor of Christ Our King Presbyterian Church in Bel Air, Maryland, where he and his wife, Jan, served for twenty-nine years before retiring in 1991. Peterson held the title of professor emeritus of spiritual theology at Regent College, British Columbia, from 1998 until his death in 2018.

ABOUT THE TYPE

This book was set in Sabon, a typeface designed by the well-known German typographer Jan Tschichold (1902–74). Sabon's design is based upon the original letter forms of sixteenth-century French type designer Claude Garamond and was created specifically to be used for three sources: foundry type for hand composition, Linotype, and Monotype. Tschichold named his typeface for the famous Frankfurt typefounder Jacques Sabon (c. 1520–80).

The Definitive Collection of Eugene H. Peterson's Teachings

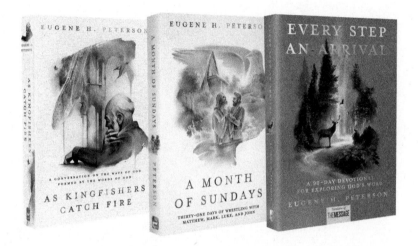

Through the life and words of Eugene H. Peterson, one of the most renowned pastors and theological teachers of our time, you'll see Jesus—and every aspect of your life—with new eyes.

"This hunger for something radical—
something so true that it burned in his bones—
was a constant in Eugene's life. His longing for
God ignited a ferocity in his soul."

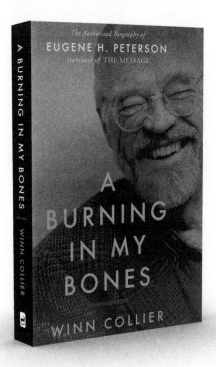

A Burning in My Bones is the essential authorized biography of
Eugene H. Peterson. Winn Collier, through exclusive interviews
and access to Eugene's personal writings, artfully reveals the
dreams, struggles, and spiritual life of the iconic American
pastor and beloved translator of *The Message*.